THE COVID BRIDE

THE
COVID
BRIDE

Lessons *in* Wedding Planning
from the Girl Who's Seen It All

SARA
LA CHAPELLE

The COVID Bride: Lessons in Wedding Planning from the Girl Who's Seen It All

Hardcover ISBN: 978-1-5445-2694-2

Paperback ISBN: 978-1-5445-2693-5

eBook ISBN: 978-1-5445-2695-9

For my wonderful husband.
Thank you for still wanting to marry me.

Contents

THE INTRODUCTION

I felt like I was cursed.

Nothing about my engagement year went according to plan. A global pandemic, unexpected loss, RSVP disasters, last-minute changes, and miscellaneous misadventures all conspired to keep me from marrying Peter. For over fourteen months, I meticulously planned for the wedding year of my dreams, only to find myself canceling and replanning events every step of the way.

You may have picked up this book because the title triggered some sort of an emotional response. Perhaps you were a COVID bride, or you know one. Maybe you just like a good wedding tale. Whatever the reason, this book is not just for those brides impacted by the pandemic, but for all newly engaged women planning a wedding and past brides who can find humor in relating to former struggles.

In a nutshell, this book serves as a guide chock full of advice I wish I had known before I was engaged. This book won't help you choose between peonies or roses, but you can always call me for that. Wedding planning is stressful enough, and I refuse to bombard you with the basic tips and tricks. Instead, I am giving you only the golden nuggets of wedding wisdom and advice you can't find on Google.

My goal is not to promote any particular vendors or retailers. In fact, although everything presented here is based on true events, I have modified the places and names to protect those involved.

Your mom, aunt, or grandma may be filled with well-intended wedding advice, but their outdated guidance can only get you so far. Sure, you can turn to your girlfriends for direction. But they most likely didn't document and reflect on a year's worth of the good, the bad, and the ugly and bind it together in a pretty book specifically for you. Although you could read every chapter in this book independently, I encourage you to follow the story to get more bang for your buck.

Global pandemic or not, planning your wedding will come with unique challenges. I hope my story will bring solace that you are **not** the only bride feeling the heavy burden of managing a wedding.

We were able to host the wedding of our dreams after hours of planning, hard work, and a little too much wine. I'll help you minimize the mishaps, avoid the true catastrophes, recover from the misfortune, and maximize the opportunities surrounding wedding planning.

You deserve a fairytale wedding. We all deserve a happily ever after.

Hang on tight,
The COVID Bride

THE BRIDE

There are plenty of women out there who have never fantasized about being proposed to by their Prince Charming. There are also plenty of women who never devoted hours talking about their future wedding before having an eligible bachelor in sight. I was **not** one of those women.

Ever since I was an awkward, lanky teenager, I would daydream about my future proposal, bachelorette party, bridal shower, wedding day, and so on. It's not my fault; from the time I was born, I was predestined to care about these traditions because of my upbringing. Thanks to my parents, I am an odd combination of sweet Southern belle mixed with tough Italian New Yorker. My dad is from L.A. (lower Alabama), and he instilled traditional values, Southern hospitality, and manners. My mother, on the other hand, is an overbearing Italian woman who began asking me in middle school when I was going to find a husband.

If my parents were to have their own catchphrases, my dad's would be, "Kill them with kindness!" and my mother's would be, "You're not getting any younger!"

Once I graduated with my MBA, my father wondered when I would be taking over the family business, and my mother and grandmother wanted to know when I would be having children. Yes, the C-word. **Children.** Having lots of children is the ultimate goal in an Italian-Catholic family.

To claim that I am the last of my friends to get married is a lie, but I have surely kept my family and friends on their toes, finally finding my match after years of unsuccessful dating. Whenever I met someone new, I would ask my grandma and mom, "How do you know when you have found **the** one?"

They would always reply with, "When you know, you know," and I hated that.

Ironically, they were correct.

THE GROOM

I first saw Peter on a private Facebook group the summer before starting graduate school. I was scrolling through the MBA Future Business Leaders page and saw Peter's face. My heart sank a little bit, and my immediate reaction was, *Oh no, this is going to be a problem for me.* Just one glance at his outdated Facebook profile picture, and I knew it would be tough to avoid taking interest in this complete stranger.

I'd made a promise to myself that I wouldn't let any man interfere with my goals. Moving to Washington, DC, for business school was my chance to start over, and falling in love **again** was totally off the table. Jumping into a relationship was the last thing I needed. I had a long list of ex-boyfriends, much like Taylor Swift, giving my hometown plenty of gossip material.

"Is she ever going to settle down?"

"I thought she was dating someone else; who is she with now?"

"I heard he's not even from the United States. Couldn't she find someone from America?"

The truth is, I have always presented myself as an independent person, yet I found myself in new relationships far too often. For once in my life, I was going to focus on myself.

Casual dating was the best I could do in my early twenties because I still didn't know what kind of man I saw myself building a future with. I have never had a **type**, so choosing a partner was like going to an all-you-can-eat buffet but being told you can only choose one dish. How could I choose just one when I love all types of food? I needed to taste all of the dishes before deciding on one to eat for the rest of my life.

When I saw Peter in person for the first time on the first day of MBA orientation, I couldn't shake the feeling of immediate attraction. I was overcome with emotions for someone I didn't even know. Instead of avoiding him, as I told myself I would, I found myself trying to get his attention or find a seat near him. Three days of MBA orientation went by, and Peter hadn't said a single word to me. Our only interaction was when Peter caught me randomly staring at him throughout the day. If he caught me looking at him once more, I would perish from embarrassment.

All of the rules I made about avoiding Peter went out the window after a week of admiring him from afar. Finally, I broke down and introduced myself, and asked for his number. Peter still hates that I technically made the first move. At least he went in for the first kiss a couple weeks later; I'll give him that.

Anyway, I just knew from the moment I saw Peter that he was **the one**. I always tell Peter that I'd hate him if he wasn't mine because I couldn't handle seeing someone so compatible with me with someone else.

After two years of dating, Peter and I got engaged in the midst of a global pandemic, and so the story begins...

THE RING

My First Engagement Ring

I was engaged for the first time when I was just nineteen.

Chase caught my eye when I was only fourteen years old, and we grew up together. He was the first **boy** I ever loved and the first person I had a somewhat adult relationship with. He was my first sleepover. His family was the first family I ever loved like my own. We met in Palm Beach at a country club my family travels to every Christmas break.

I went to a carnival with two of my girlfriends one evening, and he was there. My fourteen-year-old-self fell head over heels for his shaggy brown hair and tiny Irish nose. I ran into Chase and his friends again the next night on the beach, a common hangout spot for spoiled teenagers to make out and drink their parents' stolen vintage Dom Perignon. I was enamored by his bad boy attitude, and I was willing to do anything to get his attention. I asked for a Solo cup of champagne and pretended to drink with him.

I was a goody two-shoes back then, and my mother had taught me to **pretend** to drink so people didn't think I was weird. Her best advice was to pour my drink into plants when no one was looking or take it into the bathroom and dump it down the sink. My mom's advice always works, and it landed my girlfriends and me an invite to Chase's house party the next night. Chase and his friends were handsome, older, and so much cooler than we were. Getting invited to his party was the highlight of our trip.

When we arrived at his house for the party, we quickly learned that he wasn't just **any** member of the country club. He was country club royalty. Everyone knew Chase and his family. He had a charming older brother and a pretty younger sister. His parents were the type that allowed the kids to have as many friends over as they wanted and never acknowledged underage drinking. His family threw legendary parties and had multi-million-dollar houses, from a ranch in Montana to a Versace mansion in Italy. They owned a private island in the Bahamas and had yachts, private planes, and personal shoppers. It was unlike anything I had ever encountered.

As much as his glamorous lifestyle appealed to me, I adored Chase for who he was. I took an immediate liking to him before I knew anything about his generational wealth or bottomless trust fund. We dated long-distance throughout high school and well into college. I went to the University of Georgia; he went to the University of Alabama as a legacy of his great-grandfather, who was a founding member. The distance was brutal, but we made the five-hour drive to see each other as often as possible.

During the summer before my junior year of college, one of my best friends was in a tragic hot-air balloon accident while vacationing in Switzerland. Something went wrong with the equipment, and the intoxicated balloon operator couldn't fix it before she and her family fell out of the air. Her father passed away, and my friend, her sister, and her mother were in critical condition for months.

The news made me question the purpose of life, and I couldn't wrap my head around how God could hurt such an incredible family. When Chase heard the news, he immediately drove up to Athens, Georgia, to see me. We drank our blues away (something we did far too often together), and I told him how heartbroken I was.

"We aren't guaranteed time on this Earth. We never know when it's going to be our last day," I sobbed.

Overcome with sadness and intoxication, Chase did the one thing you should never do when you're drunk—propose! He got down on one knee, removed my everyday David Yurman ring from my middle finger, placed it on my wedding finger, and begged, "Will you marry me? I can't imagine life ending without you officially being mine."

We held each other and cried happy tears and sad tears until we finally passed out on my bed, still wearing our jeans. When we woke up in the bright morning sun, neither of us were ready to ask if the other remembered what we'd agreed to the night before. With the level of headache I was experiencing, I knew we could shake it off like we had no recollection of the night before.

By noon, I made it downstairs to brew some coffee. As I was pouring Chase a cup, he whispered, "Sara, you know I still want to marry you, right?"

We were as happy as immature young adults could be. That day, Chase called his mother with the big news. "Sara and I are engaged!" He shouted into his beat-up cell phone.

"I couldn't be happier! What kind of ring does she want? Cartier? Harry Winston?" His mother was over the moon with joy.

A complete jewelry amateur, I responded with, "I'd be happy with anything!"

"I have the perfect ring for you. Why don't I give Sara the family stone?" she offered.

I figured the family stone would be a modest one-carat diamond on a vintage thick metal band from the early 1900s. Since the family was one of the first to settle in America, they had unique heirlooms. Chase procured the family stone and officially proposed to me at my grandparents' house a week later. When I saw the family stone his mother was talking about, I was speechless. The ring had a four-carat oval diamond center stone between one-carat triangular baguettes on either side. It was bigger than any other ring I had seen before, but at the time, I still couldn't comprehend how valuable and rare it was.

Six months into the engagement, Chase and I decided it was best to go our separate ways. I called my mom to break the news. "Mom, do you think you can cancel everything? I don't think I can."

"I'm not canceling everything!" my mom snapped, hoping we would change our minds. "You call everyone."

Forced to clean up the mess I made, I fired my wedding planner and recycled the invitations. On reflection, I can see how God was preparing me for planning a wedding during a global pandemic, because this story sounds like déjà vu.

My parents lost a couple thousand dollars on deposits, but I lost my will to be seen in public. My engagement had been a **huge** deal—it was the first amongst my friends and the talk of the town. My sorority announced my engagement in front of two hundred and eighty sisters during a chapter meeting. It was announced in newspapers in Alabama, Georgia, and Florida. Everywhere I went, people I didn't even know congratulated me on my engagement.

Even though Chase was raised as a millionaire socialite, heir to the family fortune, with the world at his fingertips, he didn't want to be a part of that world. He was happiest when he was camping in the woods, free of technology and the hustle of everyday modern life. He pictured his life in Colorado, filled with outdoorsy activities, two unruly hunting dogs, and a few weathered flannel shirts.

I envisioned myself in a big house in the suburbs, PTA president, and a closet full of designer shoes. He needed a wife who was granola and easygoing, and I needed a husband who would leave for work wearing a tailored suit.

We officially ended our engagement one weekend at my college townhouse in Athens. As painful as it was to part after our seven-year love saga, the feeling was mutual. We wanted the best for each other.

I wiggled that spectacular engagement ring off my finger and mumbled, "You'll always be my first everything. I will always have love for you in my heart. I am so sorry." I did my best to not blink or tears would begin rolling down my face, making it even harder for him to leave. I stood in the kitchen and watched Chase's truck disappear down the road before I let myself cry. I didn't hear from him for an entire year, and I haven't seen him since that cold winter afternoon. His family no longer vacations in Palm Beach, so the likelihood of seeing each other again is slim.

That is the story of the first engagement ring I was given. That flawless four-carat center stone ruined my expectations of what an engagement ring should look like. Present-day me has spent hours researching fine estate accessories, and I now have a deep appreciation for jewelry, particularly diamonds.

My Second Engagement Ring

Before I ever met Peter, I thought I knew what kind of engagement ring I wanted. It would be a two- or three-carat oval center stone, VVS1 (very, very slightly included), color F or above, and an excellent cut, set in a diamond band with a seamless halo.

The second year of my MBA program, and six years after my first engagement, Peter and I started talking more seriously about a future together. Eventually, we came to the decision that we were ready to start looking for an engagement ring.

We made appointments with the finest jewelers in Washington, DC. It would cost $40,000–$50,000 to deliver the ring I wanted, and this was outside of our budget. One weekend, we took the train up to New York City and tried on engagement rings at Tiffany's and Co, Cartier, Harry Winston, and BVLGARI. The entry price was closer to $100,000 for the same two-carat oval stone set in a halo.

As two graduate students with no income, finding a ring that fit my expectations and made Peter proud was clearly going to be a challenge.

The more we shopped around, the more we realized that we needed to get creative. Years ago, I established an LLC in Georgia for an e-commerce site; I figured I could use those connections to get me in the door with diamond wholesalers. I couldn't believe I didn't think of it before! If Peter and I were able to shop for a wholesale diamond, we would save a percentage of the overall commission given to the middleman or jewelry store.

We flew to Atlanta in January of 2020 to look at stones at Atlanta's Mart. For non-Georgians, Atlanta's Mart is a massive business-to-business outlet for retail stores and boutiques to purchase items dirt cheap. In our minds, this was the solution.

Peter and I pounded the pavement of Atlanta's diamond district for two days straight, hustling and haggling with over twenty diamond wholesalers, only to find out that the stones we wanted weren't even GIA certified and most definitely a scam.

Shopping for a diamond was an emotional process, and trying to bargain for it only made me feel like we were placing a monetary value on my commitment to Peter. After two six-hour days of haggling at Atlanta's Mart, we felt slimy and exhausted. Before calling it quits, I called a jeweler in Atlanta to ask for an appointment.

We snagged the last available Sunday appointment before returning to DC.

Peter and I wore our best winter suits and set out to Manoli Fine Jewelry in Buckhead. The prices seemed reasonable, and the sales consultant was transparent about the price of their stones.

We were able to find a three-carat stone for $30,000. In DC, a comparable stone would have been priced around $50,000.

Peter and I agreed that this stone was a steal, and we would work with Manoli Fine Jewelry to purchase it. Following our appointment, we went to Cafe Collet, one of my favorite French bistros in the city, for a champagne toast to celebrate our big decision.

That evening, Peter called his parents to ask for permission to sell off a small portion of his stocks to pay for the ring. Peter's parents had set aside money for the children to use as they saw fit. Peter's sister Emily used a portion of her money for a down payment on a three-bedroom home in Los Angeles. His brother Daniel did the same thing, using a portion of the funds for a down payment on a townhouse in DC. Peter didn't see how asking for a portion of the money to use for an engagement ring would be any different. Just like his siblings, he was investing in his future.

Upon hearing Peter's request, his parents immediately shut down and refused to talk about it. Peter was upset that his parents couldn't understand the value of purchasing an engagement ring. After hunting high and low to find a fairly priced diamond ring, our engagement plans came to a screeching halt. We didn't know how to proceed.

Peter's parents didn't call him back for three days. Those three days felt like an eternity, and neither of us could catch a solid night's sleep.

I took their reaction as a personal rejection of our future engagement. I thought I was an excellent choice for a partner. I came from a good family and had a job lined up following graduation. My parents told us they would help us out by paying our rent for the first year. My dad was excited about our engagement and ensured our budget would cover as many guests as the Trelenbergs wanted to invite.

Even if I wasn't their number one choice, studies proved that married men have a fifty percent lower mortality rate than single men. To put things into perspective, daily exercise only decreases your mortality rate by twenty percent, so if I only helped their son live longer, that's enough of a win.

During those three days of silence, my mom did her best to comfort me. She told Peter and me that we could trade in her first wedding ring and use the cash to purchase the ring we wanted.

Peter's father finally broke the silence and suggested using his collection of savings bonds to purchase the ring. This was a step in the right direction, but a stack of fifty-dollar savings bonds wasn't going to cover the ring we imagined.

We were in limbo, trying to figure out what we could afford. A few days later, Peter's parents called him back and committed to giving him $5,000 to help pay for the ring. Bingo! Between the savings bonds, trading in my mother's ring, and $5,000 cash, we had enough money to purchase a ring **close** to our original design.

Peter and I had to call Manoli and let our jeweler know that the three-carat stone was out of the running. We told him our new budget, and he tried not to laugh when we asked him to keep his eye peeled for a two-carat stone with the same cut, color, and clarity.

Three weeks went by, and we got a phone call late in the morning telling us that our jeweler had found our stone.

"Here is the catch," he explained. "I need you to pay for it immediately, or else I'll have to sell it to another one of my couples on the waiting list. You're not the only ones waiting for a diamond in this price range. I can give you until the end of tomorrow."

Between our first appointment at Manoli and that phone call, the world began to shut down due to COVID19. It was the beginning of March 2020, and no one knew what was happening or how serious the virus was going to be.

Peter spent six hours in a Wells Fargo cashing his savings bonds. The bank only had standing windows, so Peter stood the entire time, signing the backs of hundreds of savings bonds with his name, social security number, and address, then waited for each bond to clear.

Peter's parents still hadn't sent him the $5,000 they'd promised, so the only money we had was the funds from the bonds. With the news of COVID, businesses in DC shut down completely, and we couldn't find a jeweler to appraise my mother's ring. Without the money from Peter's parents or the cash from my mom's ring, we couldn't pay for the diamond from Manoli. We'd move to the bottom of the waiting list for the next one, and we had no idea how long it would take to find another stone.

I jumped in the shower to clear my mind, but an idea popped into my head. I didn't even have a chance to wash the shampoo out of my hair or dry off before I threw on baggy sweatpants and a gym t-shirt.

"Peter, put your shoes on! We're running to the bank," I called as I rushed through the apartment. "Quick, we only have fifteen minutes because the bank closes at noon."

Peter didn't ask questions; he joined me as I sprinted down the streets of DC with wet, soapy hair.

"I'm going to wire you $5,000 from my savings account. I can put the rest of the diamond on my credit card, and we can sell Mom's ring once we get it appraised," I panted, out of breath.

We made it to the bank with scarcely a minute to spare, and the staff locked the front door behind us to keep out any new visitors.

Within the next few minutes, Peter had an additional $5,000 sitting in his bank account, and we could call Manoli to buy the ring. Peter received an email with the final invoice and noticed that it was $1,000 over our budget because we forgot to include sales tax.

Peter came up with the brilliant idea of shipping the engagement ring to his family's beach house in Delaware to avoid the tax. Peter called the jeweler to arrange the new shipping address and payment.

The next morning, Peter and I set out on a two-hour drive to Rehoboth Beach to wait for our precious ring. We could finally relax once we confirmed the setting design with our jeweler, modeling the ring after one of my favorite Harry Winston settings.

This time, I didn't have a hand-me-down four-carat diamond on my hand; instead, I got a respectful stone with a fantastic story.

When strangers tell me how gorgeous my engagement ring is, I can't help but laugh. I know the full story behind this symbol of love and everything Peter and I went through to get it. I will never question the level of commitment Peter made to me.

I've always believed that a man should have to make some sort of a sacrifice when buying an engagement ring, or it won't mean anything to him. Paying for an engagement ring can't feel like an everyday purchase; it should hurt his wallet a little bit. It is a commitment and an investment, and it should feel like one.

A weaker man would have quit trying to buy me the ring of my dreams just to save his ego. He would have secretly purchased a three-carat, lab-grown diamond to avoid disappointing me (nothing against lab-grown diamonds; they are a great environmentally friendly option). The right man was willing to compromise, accept help, and prove to his family that he was ready to marry, with or without their support.

Every morning, I slip on my sparkly, oval diamond with a seamless halo, knowing that I found a man who would stop at nothing to make me happy.

Engagement Ring Advice

- **Educate Yourself.** There are online resources available to teach you about diamonds, and I wouldn't skip that education process. Purchasing an engagement ring is a huge investment, and you should know what you are getting. No one wants to pay for a Mercedes, only to find out that it drives and looks like a Toyota.

- **Know the four Cs:** carat, color, clarity, and cut. This is essential information for couples purchasing a ring. If you understand the grading scale of a diamond, you are less likely to be taken advantage of. You can pay $5,000 for a one-carat diamond or $11,000 for a one-carat diamond, based on its score on the GIA scale. See the graphic below.

A BEGINNERS GUIDE
to diamond grading

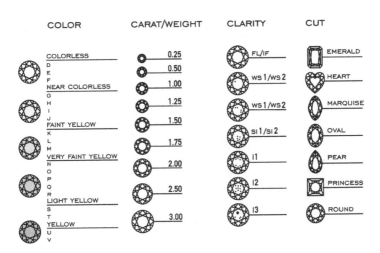

COLOR	CARAT/WEIGHT	CLARITY	CUT
COLORLESS	0.25	FL/IF	EMERALD
D	0.50		
E		WS 1/WS 2	HEART
F			
NEAR COLORLESS	1.00		
G	1.25	WS 1/WS 2	MARQUISE
H			
I	1.50		
J			
FAINT YELLOW		SI 1/SI 2	OVAL
K	1.75		
L			
M		I1	PEAR
VERY FAINT YELLOW	2.00		
N			
O			
P	2.50	I2	PRINCESS
Q			
R			
LIGHT YELLOW	3.00	I3	ROUND
S			
T			
YELLOW			
U			
V			

- **Find the right center stone before worrying about the setting.** Finding the best quality diamond that you can afford is more important than focusing on the finished product. It's complicated to select your setting if you don't know the shape or size of the center stone. Once you land on a center stone, you can browse hundreds of setting options within your budget.

- **Ask questions before you buy.** If you're lucky like we were, you might find a jeweler who allows you to trade in your diamond for the price you purchased it for and pay the difference for an upgraded stone at a later date.

- **Find the right engagement ring for you.** Not every woman wants a big diamond or even a diamond at all. You may want an emerald, a sapphire, a ruby, or just a black tattooed band—you are the only person who has to love it!

The Budget Bride

If you have family jewelry, you can convert any stone into an engagement ring by placing the stone in a custom setting. This option could save thousands of dollars on the stone alone and would cost somewhere between $1,000 and $5,000, depending on the setting you choose.

An engagement ring is an intensely personal piece of jewelry; some women want something huge and flashy; others want an unembellished or understated piece. It's essential to find something that personally fits you, whether it's a family heirloom, an environmentally conscious or ethically sourced stone, or a bespoke piece of art. Consider what you'll feel comfortable wearing every day. Starting your search with a clearly defined budget can help you avoid some of the chaos we went through. If you aren't finding rings in your price range in your area, consider exploring farther afield. The same stone, with the same GIA score, ranged from $30,000 to $100,000 in three different geographical locations.

THE PROPOSAL

The proposal is an important moment in the timeline of a couple's relationship. Rom-coms and social media fooled me into believing that my proposal would be one for the big screens. There would be some sort of fancy transportation, like a helicopter or a limousine that brought me to the rooftop of a fancy restaurant that served me the best four-course meal of my life. Or better yet, Peter would propose someplace enchanting, like overlooking the cliffs of Big Sur or in a foreign country with a professional photographer hiding in the bushes to capture the moment.

Peter almost made my over-the-top proposal fantasy come true. We planned to travel to Los Angeles to visit Peter's family and friends during spring break. He arranged an entire week of activities and dinners, and made plans to borrow his father's convertible to drive up the Pacific Coast Highway to Big Sur. I'd never been before, and I thought it would be a romantic place for an engagement.

About one month before our trip to LA, I called Peter with some news. "Hey, do you have a minute to talk?" I asked.

"Sure, I'm driving home from campus. What's up?" Peter mumbled through his speakerphone.

"Well, I think I might have to cancel our trip to LA. I know you've been looking forward to it, but I have the option to earn an extra credit that week if I sign up for an international real estate course. I'd be learning about the real estate market in South America," I informed him.

Peter was understanding. "I know you need an extra credit, and this sounds like a great opportunity."

"Yep, it's just one week. We're visiting Chile and Argentina. There are some readings I need to catch up on, but it should be pretty painless," I went on about the class. "After the trip, I have to submit a paper."

"That's awesome. I've always wanted to visit South America. I wish you could still come to LA." Peter sounded disappointed. "I guess we'll have to get engaged in DC."

Two weeks before my trip to South America, my dad called to discuss the details. He was concerned that South America was dangerous, and he would feel safer if I bought Peter a ticket to come along.

"What a great idea!" I told my dad. I was actually thinking, *Now our proposal plans are back on, and Peter can pop the question in Chile or Argentina! How cool would that be?*

I'm not sure what reality I was living in because, at this point, Peter and I had only tried on diamonds and had yet to purchase one. We were still waiting to hear back from Manoli if they could find an oval stone in our price range. I foolishly thought Peter could overnight a finished ring the second we found a stone.

The week before spring break, COVID cases started popping up all over the map. The United States and South America closed their borders the day of our scheduled flight. Peter and I went from having the most amazing plans to no plans. We ended up spending our spring break wearing puffer jackets and sweatpants in Rehoboth Beach, Delaware, waiting for the ring we eventually purchased.

We waited for two weeks for the ring to finally arrive. I was the one to sign for the FedEx package, but I'd promised Peter I wouldn't peek. Since nothing about our upcoming engagement was a surprise, I wanted the ring to be.

Peter was dying to show off his first really big purchase. He sent cell phone photos to his brother Daniel, only to receive a less-than-excited response. Daniel had been dating his girlfriend Sophia for a couple of years and felt blindsided by our rather quick engagement. Peter and his brother are fundamentally different and like very different women.

Lucky for me, Peter isn't turned off by my feminine, ex-pageant queen style of spray tans, lip liner, the color pink, and an excuse to wear fake hair (lashes or extensions, you name it). Daniel, on the other hand, is attracted to the highly educated, political type who pokes fun at the suitcase of beauty products I can't seem to part with (even for a quick weekend trip). Sophia is serious; I am Southern. She grew up going to Coachella; I grew up going to Country Fair. She's California cool; I have no chill.

Our pre-proposal was off to a bad start with what felt like a lack of enthusiasm from Peter's family. My first engagement was a huge mistake, and I wanted things to be perfect this go around.

During two weeks of waiting for the ring in Rehoboth Beach, the COVID spread worsened. Our MBA classes shifted online for the rest of the semester. With this newfound freedom, and the ring burning a hole in Peter's pocket, we decided to take the fourteen-hour drive to Peachtree City, Georgia, to quarantine with my parents until we figured out what was going to happen with COVID.

When we arrived at my parents' house, my mother made us strip down on the front porch, handed us towels, and told us to take a hot shower to avoid spreading potential COVID germs. Only then could we move freely about the house. We had no idea that we would be bunking with my parents for the next six months. Once I felt settled at home, I was no longer in a rush for Peter to propose. We had the ring, and we both wanted to wait for the madness to lessen so we could celebrate with family and friends. March turned into April, and it looked like there was no end in sight with COVID.

Peter decided on a backyard proposal with string lights and a bamboo pathway, but his amateur architectural skills resulted in materials that didn't measure out correctly. He called my best friend, Vivienne, to help plan a worthy backyard engagement.

Vivienne helped Peter put together a picnic that would have made Parisians proud. She set out two plush blankets and covered the corners in fresh spring bouquets from her mother's garden. She set up an old-fashioned picnic basket with a couple bottles of Veuve Clicquot and set out trays of homemade French pastries and a charcuterie board.

The strangest part of the proposal was knowing that it was going to happen. In order to get me to wear something without an elastic waistband (the early pandemic was a dark time), Peter had to outright announce the night he would propose.

Because of quarantine, we hadn't gone anywhere other than the grocery store, and my parents were our only form of social interaction for over a month.

I got ready in my childhood bedroom and painted my own nails with an expired bottle of OPI Passion. I never imagined I would be doing either of those activities before getting engaged. When Peter was ready, he escorted me from my bedroom to the picture-perfect picnic.

He was so nervous I could feel him trembling. I don't remember what he said to me outside on the picnic blanket, but I started to cry. I wasn't even caught off guard, and I was still weeping. For a girl who never cries, my tears of happiness were everything I needed to feel to remember that moment forever.

After he slipped that oval diamond on my finger, we headed toward the back porch to show my parents. I couldn't stop staring at my new ring. When we got there, I saw my grandparents for the first time in almost six months, and that's when I really started to bawl.

I didn't think the evening would be filled with any surprises, but I was wrong. My parents relaxed our quarantine to let my grandparents, my future maid of honor Vivienne and her fiancé Blake, and my brother dine with us outside to celebrate.

Vivienne and Blake captured the evening with their professional camera, and the rest of the evening was filled with laughter and joy between family, close friends, lots of cake, and even more champagne.

My proposal was not in a foreign country or overlooking breathtaking cliffs. It was not even in another state. Our proposal took place in my parents' backyard in Peachtree City,

Georgia, but it was exactly the proposal we needed at the moment. It's okay if your proposal isn't exotic or over-the-top, as long as it's real and thoughtful.

Proposal Advice

- **Don't let society influence your timeline.** Society (or other people in your life) may have a perception of when or how you should get engaged. Life is too short to wait for the right time, the right ring, or the right place to propose. Far too often, I hear couples say, "I'm waiting for a promotion," or, "We need to pay off our student loans first," or whatever excuse is holding them back. When Peter proposed, he didn't even have a job lined up. He didn't propose with the massive three-carat diamond we originally picked out, and we didn't get engaged in Big Sur or South America. None of that mattered to us. We were ready to make it official. Waiting for Peter to afford a bigger diamond or having a Hollywood-style proposal wouldn't have made us any happier.

- **Embrace where you are in life and your relationship.** Once you get engaged, you have the rest of your lives to strive for a house, international vacations, or a healthy savings account. Most importantly, you have the **rest of your lives to grow together.**

The Budget Bride

Take a page out of our proposal book and DIY the entire event. The amount of decorating you can achieve with grocery store flowers and borrowed props (like picnic blankets and vases) is impressive. Instead of hiring a professional photographer for hundreds of dollars, ask a friend or family member to capture the moment for you.

For photos, go to
www.thecovidbridebysara.com/post/proposal.

THE FIRST
WEDDING PLANNER

Many brides opt to not hire a wedding planner, but as organized as I am, I still wanted the expertise and guidance from someone experienced who could assist with the entire year of nuptial events.

I interviewed potential planners before falling down the planning rabbit hole. I wanted to find a talented planner, someone I could trust, and someone I'd enjoy spending time with over the next fourteen months. Whoever I hired needed to be excellent with budgeting and keeping track of expenses, because we know that's not my strong suit. Lastly, since I wanted my wedding to be unique, whoever I hired had to be creative and present ideas out of the ordinary.

Like a true business request for proposal, I sent an email to the top ten wedding planners in the Metro-Atlanta area with my scope of work and asked for an interview to hear their best pitches.

In back-to-back Zoom meetings, I interviewed well-known planners, expensive planners, budget-friendly planners, and planners with fire social media feeds. I needed to get the lay of the land before making my decision. After the interviews and final quotes, I compiled a list of pros and cons for my top two choices.

I had to choose between two wonderful options. Planner A, Bellani Events, was a highly regarded wedding planning company that I had seen in *The Atlantan Magazine*, *Jezebel*, and *The Knot*. Jenna was the lead planner assigned to my event, and I loved her energy. Her work was worthy of the numerous features she received in bridal publications. All positive reviews, except for a quote that startled me. It would be around $14,000 for her for just the wedding day! As impressed as I was, I feared I'd be **just another girl** to her.

Planner B, Somethin' Blue Events, was more reasonably priced and was willing to fulfill all of my extra requests. For a complete wedding package, Somethin' Blue sent me a proposal for $6,800, which felt like a bargain compared to Bellani Events. When talking with Madison from Somethin' Blue, I felt at ease expressing my preferences and expectations. I felt like she had my back, but maybe I was blindsided by the feeling of making a new girlfriend.

The sound financial choice, coupled with the way Madison made me feel, encouraged me to hire her company to assist with my wedding year. I met Madison for the first time in person (outside and six feet apart) in April 2020, thirteen months before our preferred wedding date. I was eager to start designing the engagement party my parents wanted to host in their backyard. Madison helped me hire every vendor, including photography, catering, entertainment, tent, chairs, and florals. One by one, we began crossing off items needed for the engagement party.

Madison and I talked almost every day. She would send me long emails, keeping me in the loop. Each week, she would check in with a "do now, do next, and do later" timeline.

Within a few months, we were able to nail down the big vendors for my wedding, too.

Madison and I worked hand in hand until Christmas break. We were pushing to finish as much as we could before the new year. Before I left for my annual trip to Palm Beach, Madison sent me one of her detailed emails with tasks to complete over the holiday. I replied to her email confirming the next steps, and we set a meeting for the Monday after the trip to touch base.

I had no idea that **that** email would be the last communication I would ever receive from her. To this day, I still don't know where Madison is or how she's doing. Madison, if you're reading this, please call me!

Wedding Planner Advice

- **Interview at least three contenders.** When you interview them, make sure you ask the same questions, such as:

    - What is the largest event budget you have managed?
    - How many guests is your ideal event?
    - What sets you apart from other wedding planners?

- Do you meet with your brides on a weekly/monthly basis?
- What is your best method for communication?
- Make your list of questions in advance and reflect on what will matter most to you from a wedding planner.

- **Look at their portfolio.** It is critical to make sure their aesthetic is in line with yours.

- **Don't reveal too much.** When interviewing wedding planners, try not to reveal too much about your budget or your guest count. You don't want these factors to influence the meeting. In the initial interview, wedding planners should be answering **your** questions, not the other way around.

- **Hire someone with skillsets that differ from yours.** Just like in our professional careers, it's smart to arrange a team with different talents for the best results. If you are a design guru but hate scheduling, hire a planner who is more focused on event logistics and less concerned with creating a color palette.

- **Don't automatically hire the most expensive planner.** The adage, "you get what you pay for," does not always apply in this situation. A high-ticket planner won't necessarily be the most involved. It comes down to finding a person you trust with the most important day of your life.

The Budget Bride

A lot of churches and reception venues have event coordinators. If you book a venue with an in-house coordinator, consider opting out of a wedding planner to save money. You can purchase a wedding planning notebook/calendar from Etsy or Amazon to ensure you are completing all essential tasks within the best time frame.

THE
ENGAGEMENT PARTY

In December 2019 (four months before our engagement),
Peter asked for and received my father's blessing. In anticipation of a shiny new ring on my finger by graduation, I began
preparing our engagement celebration.

My mother had waited twenty-six years for an eligible bachelor to ask for my hand in marriage, so she was ready to hold
the best engagement party in our honor. My father was equally
thrilled to host an engagement party because it was finally an
excuse for him to hire The Willy Banks Band to perform in
his backyard. The Willy Banks Band plays up and down the
Florida panhandle, and my parents fell in love with the band
over the years of spending our summers at the beach. Their
music reminds them of outdoor concerts with the family.

My father was the true catalyst for planning the engagement
party. Before New Year's Eve, he had already reached out to
the band to ask for their availability over the summer, keeping
in mind that our engagement party would take place during

the band's busiest season. The band's coordinator presented only one open weekend in June. My dad pulled the trigger and mailed them a deposit. That one available weekend would be the date of our engagement party, and we would find a way to hammer out the rest of the details at a later date.

Booking a band before I had a ring on my finger was a risk considering Peter and I only seriously dated for six months before making the decision to get engaged. We had dated on and off for a year prior, and our love anthem could have been Katy Perry's "Hot and Cold." In the worst-case scenario, Peter and I wouldn't be engaged by then, and we could parlay the event into my graduation party, honoring my master's degree.

My mother and I assembled a detailed invite list for the event. My list consisted of seventy-five family members and friends and provided equal invitations on Peter's side. In total, we expected an event with one hundred and fifty guests.

The majority of Peter's friends date back to his college days at the University of Southern California. No one from Peter's invite list had ever visited Georgia; layovers at Hartsfield-Jackson International Airport don't count! I wanted to host an event that would capture the sweet Southern charm of Georgia.

People who have never been to Georgia have misconceptions of what it is like to grow up in the South, especially those living in California or New York. People from either state tend to believe only two cities matter, Los Angeles and New York City. Everything else is a flyover state with the exception of their pretentious ski towns frequented in winter or their exclusive summer retreats. It's Palm Springs for the LA crowd and the Hamptons or Nantucket for New Yorkers (if you're reading this and have a house in the Hamptons, please invite me because I've always wanted to go. I can pack an all-white ensemble, sip rosé, and lounge poolside with supermodels and Manhattan's elite).

Atlanta has no clout when it comes to national recognition as a wonderful city to reside. We have an attractive skyline, the Atlanta Braves, the Hawks, the Falcons, the Georgia Aquarium, MLK's birthplace, the Beltline, and underrated restaurants. Georgia is known for being part of the Bible Belt, as well as its second amendment supporters, fried food, peaches, peanuts, and the Masters golf tournament.

While all those things are a part of Georgia, the state has a rich culture and Southern hospitality. In order to showcase a little slice of the South, I began organizing a Southern-vintage themed engagement party. I began the design process by pulling together a book of imagery from Pinterest and Google.

I wanted the overall feeling to be lively with the use of textured flowers, various greenery, and vibrant colors. The event would be elegant yet fun. Keeping in mind that our wedding design would be more sophisticated with a muted color scheme, our engagement party would be bursting with color. The palette I put together included a deep violet, a soft Georgia peach, bold magenta, royal navy, and a pop of teal.

Madison was still in the picture, so she and I devoted several afternoons to designing the party layout. Guests would enjoy cocktail hour under the back porch and around the pool deck. The porch would have a few high tops with floral arrangements, and the porch's big white columns would be draped in luscious greenery. My mother had planted a mix of magnificent spring flowers surrounding the pool, and our hydrangea bushes would be at the peak of bloom. Around the pool deck would be more high-top tables and a white bar festooned with ivy on the front and featuring our neon sign, *The Trelenbergs*.

We rented a garden-style, open-air white tent, a black and white dance floor, and a decent-sized stage for the band. After cocktail hour, guests could make their way to the tent and find a seat at one of the circle tables draped in peach tablecloths and adorned with colorful floral arrangements. I rented the cross-back wooden chairs commonly used for rustic weddings. The tables would be set with clear and gold-rimmed plates, gold flatware, and colorful crystal goblets.

On the side of the tent, we would have a buffet and second bar serving our signature cocktail. The buffet would serve a Southern heart attack: deviled eggs, artisan cheese with crackers, potato salad, cucumber salad, Waldorf salad, BBQ sliders, Carolina chicken, macaroni and cheese, and home-style cornbread.

The engagement party I planned was flawless across the board. It would be as nice as my wedding but on a smaller scale. It was my first chance to host Peter's family and friends, and I wanted to hold an event that would represent us and our special year.

I couldn't believe how real our engagement started to feel as I put more effort into this event. For the first time, I felt like I had a suitable outlet to channel my creative energy.

By mid-April, I knew I needed to postpone the engagement party we intended to hold in June. I couldn't be the jerk who hosted an engagement party when friends of ours postponed their weddings due to COVID. On a positive note, the news media anticipated COVID would dramatically decline in the hot summer months. With this in mind, I attempted to reschedule our party for August.

I contacted all ten vendors servicing the event, asking for their August availability. The only date that the majority of our vendors could make was August eighth. Unfortunately, The Willy Banks Band already had a gig that night and couldn't acquiesce to our request. It was either try to salvage the fifty percent down payments we had sent to our vendors or sacrifice the money and wait for my dad's favorite band.

To my father's dismay, we ended up switching the party to August eighth and only lost the down payment for the band. Madison championed another popular band in the Atlanta wedding circuit as a replacement. Luckily, The Georgia Band was available for our new date.

I tore open all one hundred handwritten, stamped envelopes with our engagement party invitation inside. I crossed off our original date and RSVP deadline with a black Sharpie and wrote in our new dates as neatly as I could. I readdressed each envelope by hand for the second time and popped them in the mailbox. There was no turning back now!

Over the summer months leading up to the event, Georgia opened outdoor dining and became less strict with gathering policies. Regardless of the lax atmosphere, COVID cases were still on the rise, and there was no vaccination expected for months. Peter and I were still living with my parents in July, and one morning, two weeks before the engagement party, my dad expressed his concerns about hosting the event.

"I think you need to cancel the party. I'm uneasy hosting an event with that many people," my dad stated.

"Dad, we're going to lose all of our deposits! It's too late to cancel it now. The event is going to be entirely outside. Can I just let people know that it's okay if they don't feel comfortable coming?" I dreaded the idea of canceling after all of the effort I had put into rescheduling.

"A large portion of our guests are over the age of fifty. I just had a friend pass away from COVID. We can't throw an event with everything going on. It's insensitive and too risky," he insisted.

"Can we have an event for just Peter's and my friends?" I pleaded, desperate to connect with this group I had already missed out on meeting in the past.

"Sara, we need to cancel the event." He put his foot down. "My guests will feel obligated to come, and that's not right. I don't care about the money at this point. We can reschedule it for a later date if you want."

"It was so much work rescheduling everything the first time," I whined, visibly upset. "It's fine; I'll just cancel it."

After the conversation with my dad, I drafted a text message to inform everyone I'd invited about our decision to cancel. I reached out to our vendors to share the news and attempt to salvage what credits I could put toward the wedding. We could not get back the money we'd already invested in the engagement party, but it was more important to focus my energy on the wedding and let this event go.

I was hopeful that the rest of our wedding would go according to plan. My dad was right to cancel the event because the last thing Peter and I needed was to kick off our engagement year with a super-spreader event. Little did we know, it wouldn't be socially acceptable to hold any sort of event for another ten months.

Engagement Party Advice

- **Know when it's best to cut your losses and move on.** Sometimes knowing when to quit is harder than the decision to push forward. I am not a quitter, so throwing in the towel with this event was bitter for me. This can apply to a job, a friendship, or even a romantic relationship. If you have done everything in your power to make something come together, yet the universe refuses to align, maybe it's a sign to let go.

- **Have fun with your engagement party.** Take a less serious approach with this event! Incorporate colors, styles, foods, or a theme that you love but wouldn't necessarily choose for your wedding. Who says you can't have a Hawaiian-themed engagement party and serve poke bowls if it's special to you?

The Budget Bride

Instead of hiring a handful of event vendors for an engagement party, consider taking care of the food or floral arrangements yourself. I recently signed up for a Costco membership and learned how to place custom floral orders in advance. I made twelve wondrous centerpieces with pink mums, blush roses, and greenery for only one hundred dollars. This would have been closer to $2,000 if I went with a florist.

THE BRIDESMAID PROPOSAL

It was a no-brainer for me to ask thirteen of my closest friends to be a part of my bridal party. I've been lucky to make girlfriends easily because of my feminine nature and my girl's girl personality type.

When asking bridesmaids whether or not they want to be a part of the wedding, it is a Southern tradition to hand-deliver (or ship UPS Priority) a bridesmaid proposal, which is essentially a present with a heartfelt letter.

Being a bridesmaid in the South is a **huge** responsibility and an even bigger expense. It would be wrong to expect that your best friends want to willingly dedicate their paid-time-off days to attend your bachelorette and wedding weekend, plus a minimum of four weekends to attend (and host) bridal showers, bridal teas, or shop for your wedding gown. Don't forget that you are asking your bridesmaids to spend their hard-earned cash on a heinous bridesmaid gown they will never wear again (I promise they will not alter it into a cocktail dress after the wedding, no matter how much they claim they will).

With all of that in mind, we Southern belles like to give our friends a gift that shows a token of appreciation for everything they will be doing for us, should they accept the title of bridesmaid. I knew I wouldn't be skimping on any bridal activities or events, so I needed to come up with a gift that my girlfriends would love.

In my wedding workshop, a guest room at my parents' home converted to house all things wedding, my mom and I assembled thirteen high-quality white gift boxes with a silk ribbon. We prepared each box with white and gold confetti before filling them to their maximum capacity with goodies.

During the ordering process, the wedding workshop was covered in gold and white paper confetti and overflowed with boxes from Nordstrom, Etsy, and Amazon. It looked like I was filling orders for an e-commerce website.

Deciding on products that my girlfriends would actually use took time and thought. Twelve bridesmaids (and one junior bridesmaid) meant shopping for thirteen very different personality types. After much thought and consideration, I splurged on a pair of gold earrings they could wear for the wedding and then filled in the rest of the box with self-care items.

Each bridesmaid box contained a NARS natural shade lipstick, an ORGANICS face mask, Better than Sex Mascara, some of my favorite productivity sticky notes, a sparkly Swarovski crystal pen, a champagne tumbler, and an acrylic jewelry box to hold the gold earrings. Lastly, I added a handwritten letter asking each friend to be my bridesmaid. Each girlfriend had a part in my journey to Peter, and I wanted to specifically acknowledge how each of them changed my life.

My mom and I successfully assembled thoughtful and tasteful bridesmaid boxes. Over the next few weeks, I either hand-delivered the proposals or shipped them to my Out-of-town bridesmaids. Fortunately for me, all of my girlfriends said **yes!**

For more photos, go to
www.thecovidbridebysara.com/post/bmproposal

Bridesmaid Proposal Advice

- **Don't assume your girlfriends are in a place in their lives to be a bridesmaid.** One of my original bridesmaids backed out of the wedding only five months beforehand. I was never mad at her, and we are still friends today. Being a part of a wedding is emotional and time-consuming, and sometimes your friends may be at a point in life where they need to focus their attention on other things. That is okay!

- **Be flexible with potential changes to your bridesmaid party.** One of my best friends from Florida, Katie, joined the bridal party during the bachelorette weekend. I should have asked her from the start, but things ended up turning out exactly how they should have. In the end, I still had thirteen bridesmaids. Fortunately for everyone, the girl who backed out of the wedding shipped her bridesmaid gown to Katie, and it even fit. Talk about a peaceful and understanding friendship!

The Budget Bride

There are so many ways to reduce the price per bridesmaid proposal with a few basic swaps. Instead of delivering your gift in a box, you can use a high-quality gift bag and tissue paper, especially if delivering it in person. When ordering your goodies, search department store sales online. I was able to snag luxe beauty products for twenty-five percent off!

You could choose to go with a smaller wedding party. This can be a tough decision to make. If you have several friends whom you want to be part of your big day, you could ask some of them to take on other essential roles that come with a smaller commitment on their end. These roles include handing out wedding programs, ushering guests to seats, giving a speech at the rehearsal dinner, or sharing a religious or personal reading at the ceremony.

THE GUEST LIST

One of the first questions a bride-to-be must ask herself is, "Do I want a small wedding or a big wedding?" Most women already know the answer immediately, though sometimes budget or family expectations impact the final decision.

I have always thought a small, intimate wedding would be nice, but it was not realistic for me. Since I am the only girl in my immediate family, this was the one chance my parents would have to host a wedding. I have two brothers who are five and eight years older than me, both single, with no plans to marry. After the past year of wedding shenanigans, I don't blame them!

Creating a guest list was an emotional process, or maybe I just made it one. A bride must think about all of the people she has known throughout her life and decide whether or not they are worthy of attending her special day.

The odd thing about creating a guest list is the unexpected desire to invite people who were a notable part of your life, even if you no longer keep in touch. Therefore, creating a guest list cannot be done in a vacuum. Brides need either a parent or close friend to be their sounding board and keep them rational. *No, you may not invite your first ballet teacher, whom you only keep in touch with on Facebook!*

I can almost guarantee that most brides do not complete their list in one day. I kept thinking of more people I wanted to invite a week or two after drafting my initial list. I would wake up in the middle of the night and jot down former teachers and coaches who came to mind.

Despite the advice of, "invite whomever you want, it's your wedding," I found my parents' input essential, especially since they were going to be paying for it. Shortly after Peter proposed, my dad hosted a little family meeting with my mother and me to discuss how much money he had set aside for my wedding. My dad was adamant on us not going over the budget. As an incentive for me to not go overboard, Dad told me that Peter and I could keep whatever money we didn't spend from the budget to use toward a down payment on a house.

With that knowledge, Peter and I grappled with the idea of how we could hold a small, inexpensive wedding. The notion of a small wedding sounded really enticing. At the time, Peter was my stay-at-home fiancé, studying for the bar exam (which had been postponed by several months).

Before deciding how many guests to invite, I thought it would be reasonable for the two of us to list out all of our family members and bridal party. I opened a fresh Google spreadsheet and began listing my family members first. For the record, that particular spreadsheet has been through six iterations to reformat the data based on our various vendors' requests.

Pro-tip: Use a different column for name, street address, city, state, and zip code. It will make your life easier in the long run!

My initial guest list with my parents, grandparents, aunts, uncles, and first cousins totaled fifty-three guests. After writing down everyone in my immediate family, I added my thirteen bridesmaids and a space for each of them to invite a plus one. Between my immediate family and bridesmaids, my guest list was already at seventy-seven. If I gave Peter the same number of invites, our guest list would total one hundred and fifty-four guests.

It was out of the cards for us to have a small wedding, considering our friends, my dad's work partners, and my mother's neighborhood friends weren't even on the list. Following this realization, I sat down with my parents to get feedback on the guest list. After all, my personality is "go big or go home," and I wasn't about to strip away my mother's only chance to plan a wedding.

In meeting with my parents, I noticed my mom was adamant about inviting neighborhood friends with whom she hadn't spoken in years. I came up with a rule of thumb that if she had to look up someone's phone number on Facebook, they would not get an invite. Although it was a useful rule, most of my mother's neighborhood friends failed my Facebook test but still ended up on the list.

The Trelenberg addresses were more challenging to acquire. If it weren't for Peter's mom, he wouldn't have added more than twenty guests to the list. In the end, I'm pleased to note that we had equal numbers of guests.

After three months, the guest count totaled three hundred and twenty-five. It was much larger than I anticipated, but I thought it would be manageable. Studies show that roughly seventeen percent of guests will decline a wedding invitation, so there was no way we would be responsible for hosting an event of this size.

Keeping up with our large guest list unexpectedly became a full-time job. When COVID began spreading, our family and friends relocated across the country for different reasons. Roughly half of our guest list changed addresses at some point during our engagement year. In some cases, guests stayed in another location for an extended period, only to move again. Over the course of a year, I had collected three different addresses for some of my friends: their original address before the pandemic, a temporary address where they stayed during the strict lock-down, and a third address when they found a new place to relocate permanently.

It was a miracle our guests received our save-the-date card or invitation. There are a lot of reasons so many people relocated during COVID. There was an immense fear amongst people living in cities, where the spread of COVID was initially most prevalent. Like a handful of our guests, Peter and I moved out of our tiny Washington, DC, apartments and retreated to my parents' house in the suburbs for six months before finding an apartment of our own. We had planned to move to Atlanta after graduation, but we ended up relocating five months earlier than anticipated. While we had originally intended on being city dwellers, the suburbs became our permanent address.

It felt safer to live in a single-family home rather than a busy apartment where hundreds of people reside. Even if you were strictly quarantining in your apartment, there was still a fear of catching COVID in the lobby or elevator.

Some people moved because of their jobs. A significant number of our friends relocated during the pandemic because their jobs no longer tied them to an office. Telecommuting provided people the flexibility to live where they actually wanted to live, rather than staying near their offices. People moved everywhere and anywhere.

Another thing I noticed amongst my friends was how quickly COVID changed us. The pandemic turned us from cool urban professionals into antisocial suburban homeowners with pets. Before the pandemic, my friend group was young, hip, and thriving in the city. The older millennials were more than happy to sacrifice square footage in their apartments for a buzzing city lifestyle. The city lifestyle made it effortless for us to go to work, attend an early morning workout class, and meet up with friends for happy hour.

With the pandemic, the amenities that drew us to city life were no longer available. Dining was closed, concerts were canceled, gyms attempted to train virtually, and even public parks were roped off to prevent group gatherings. In addition to the shutdowns, 2020 was a year of civil unrest. Whenever I turned on my TV, there was a protest, a city takeover, a shooting, or news on the increase in crime rates across the country. It was an overwhelming year for everyone.

These demographic trends applied to half of our guest list. During our engagement year, an average of twenty percent of our guests did not receive our save-the-date card, engagement party invite, bridal shower invite, or the wedding invitation itself!

Having a big guest list seemed like something I could manage, but I had not anticipated so many address changes over the twelve months following the list's creation. Planning this wedding had so many moving pieces and changes to accommodate for COVID, and this was just another piece of the puzzle that caused much stress and drama.

Guest List Advice

- **Continually check in with your guests to see if their address is correct.** I advise doing so at the twelve-month, six-month, and three-month marks. Invitations are expensive, and you want to make sure people are actually getting them!

- **Make sure you and your significant other are on the same page about the guests you're inviting to the wedding.** It was too late when I found out Peter invited his old roommate (who happened to be a girl and was secretly in love with him). Before we were engaged, she and her boyfriend unfollowed me on social media. Nothing says "I want to be invited to your wedding" quite like unsubscribing from my life!

- **Make an A-list and a B-list.** My wedding planner, Madison, advised me not to do this, and I regret listening to her advice. If you have a budget to stick to and don't know the final charge per head (which can fluctuate as the big day approaches), it is better to divide your list into two. As people on your A-list respectfully decline, you can invite more guests without having to worry about the budget.

- **Do not assume the price per person is just what it costs to have a seated dinner or buffet per head.** This is my most painfully hard-earned piece of advice on this subject. When building our guest list, we did not consider all of the additional expenses associated with each guest. Budget for alcohol per person (per hour), table setting rentals (plate, charger, flatware, glasses), linens and floral arrangements per table, and even slices of cake. Can you believe we were charged eight dollars per person to cut the cake? When I added it up, I was not risking the loss of two hundred and fifty dollars per person; I was risking a loss of $1,000 per person who RSVPed but didn't show up!

The Budget Bride

When making a guest list, work backward with your budget. If you have an event budget of $10,000, set aside seventy-five percent of your budget for the venue and vendors. Now, take your remaining budget and divide it by the ideal number of guests. Let's say you want fifty guests. $2,500/50 shakes out to $50 per person for food and drink on the wedding day.

THE VENUE

At the ripe age of twenty-one, I was invited to a black-tie charity event by a guy I would eventually date. I'd been to many black-tie events and knew this was my chance to thrive and impress him. I slipped on a silver mermaid gown, donned three-inch heels, and curled my long, thick hair. When we pulled up to this enchanting French-looking estate with ivy growing up on the stone walls, I didn't recognize where I was. But then it dawned on me that I had never seen the front of this building, and I knew exactly where I was!

At the time, I lived in an apartment within walking distance of Peachtree Park, the Central Park of Atlanta. I liked to walk the park for exercise, taking a few laps around the soccer fields closest to Peachtree Street.

From the backside of the soccer fields, I could see an imposing building with white columns. It was Braxton Country Club or BCC. Founded in the late 1800s as a gentlemen's club, BCC is one of Atlanta's most exclusive private clubs. With a minimal internet footprint and rare media presence, the club has always been a mystery to me.

Regardless of my little functional knowledge of the club, I always dreamed of being a member one day. It seemed like a little slice of Paris in the city. By thirty years old, I'd wear a white tennis outfit and drop my children off at the Brookhaven International School in my silver Mercedes G-Wagon. I'd spend the afternoon at the club engaging in light physical activity, lunch with the ladies, and then peel off for a few hours of freelance writing for *Southern Living*, *Town and Country*, and *The Atlantan*. As I walked past the club every evening after work, I could imagine myself living that life.

As my date and I pulled up to BCC, I was overjoyed to finally experience what was inside this mysterious estate. When I stepped through the double French doors to an ornate hallway filled with an art collection fit for a queen, I felt at home. The hallway led to the grand foyer with high ceilings, lots of marble, French molding, and gold everything. Each room got better and better. Finally, my date and I entered the main ballroom, and my heart skipped a beat. The ballroom had white columns down either side, incredible windows, and chandeliers that did not disappoint.

I had only known my date for a couple of months, but I couldn't help but say, "I will get married here," out loud. And that was that. I'd decided BCC would be where I would host the wedding of my dreams.

Fast forward six years to December 2019, when Peter joined my family on our annual Christmas vacation. He had plans to ask my dad for his blessing, even though they had only met twice before.

One morning, Peter and my father went fishing around five in the morning, and by eight, my father caught his first sailfish of the day. My father is a huge fisherman, so this put him in an excellent mood. Peter decided that the best time to ask to marry me was while Dad was on a fishing high. Peter told me later that he was so nervous he was shaking but mustered up the courage to ask. My father is a warm guy and went in for a hug.

My mom and I patiently waited for the boys to return from fishing, already knowing what Peter had in mind. When the boys returned home, they were both cheerful, which meant I could proceed with wedding arrangements, even without an official engagement.

I asked my father if he knew anyone from BCC who could sponsor us so we could host our wedding reception there.

"Sure, I know a few people. I'll ask around for you," my dad offered.

That very day, I presented my dad with three possible dates in May that would do. I knew I wanted a spring wedding because Atlanta gets too hot during the summer. May is also my grandmother's birth month, and this would be the ultimate birthday present for her.

December 2019, a year and a half before our preferred date, my dad fired off an email to get the ball rolling. He connected us with a colleague who happily agreed to sponsor us. And just like that, we **thought** we confirmed our wedding date at BCC.

Four months later, Peter and I were engaged, and we still hadn't heard from BCC. We were concerned because we had already sent out save-the-date cards reserving May 8, 2021, for our wedding.

By this point, the COVID pandemic forced BCC to shut their doors and postpone their monthly board meetings where they discussed the upcoming social calendar. After months of being closed, BCC told us that they would reconvene in July (only ten months before our planned date). Until their next board meeting on July nineteenth, Peter and I would not know whether or not our reservation for the venue was official.

On an ordinary afternoon in July, Madison sent me a text message that just read, "call me," and my heart sank. Madison had been involved with weddings at BCC before and previously worked with Hannah, their lead event coordinator. Madison was just as anxious as we were about the reservation for our date, so she reached out to Hannah to check on the status of our request.

"Hey, Sara, I was talking with Hannah about reserving May eighth, and she told me that the club did not have your request on their agenda for their next meeting. Are you sure you completed the application?" Madison asked.

"Application?" I asked, perplexed. "There wasn't an application. My dad's colleague copied me in an email requesting the date with the head of events. Was there something else I needed to do?"

"Yes, your sponsor was supposed to fill out an application for you and Peter," Madison said. "Did you submit your letter asking the board for permission to use their club? They require a letter from the couple and a recommendation letter from the sponsoring member."

"A recommendation letter? No! I had no idea we needed to include this! We didn't submit an application either." I began to panic.

"Yes, apparently BCC is particular about who they allow to use their ballroom. I've never gone through this process before. The last time I did a wedding there, the bride was a member. Hannah told us not to be disappointed if they didn't approve our application. The club commonly refuses sponsor requests," Madison said.

After we hung up the phone, I ran upstairs to my computer and began drafting a letter on behalf of Peter and myself. With our wedding date only ten months away by the time our application would be considered, I needed to write a letter the board could not refuse. It would be impossible to find another venue less than a year away; May was already a busy wedding month, and many spring 2020 brides rescheduled their weddings for a year later.

Over the next few weeks, I refreshed my email several times a day, waiting for a message from BCC. A month later, I finally got the approval I was waiting for. Peter and I would be allowed to use the club on May eighth for our wedding. However, the exclusive club was hesitant because of my social media presence, blog, and budding wedding e-commerce business. The board expressed that neither my guests nor I could share any information, photos, or tag the country club on social media. For someone who **loves** sharing my life on social media, this was a huge bummer. No two-page spread in the *Atlantan Magazine*, no mention in the *Peachtree City Daily Journal*, no feature in *The Knot*, and no blog posts?

I agreed to their requests because, after seven months of waiting to hear back from the venue of my dreams, I was finally in! It would be another six months before Peter and I would realize we wouldn't be holding our reception at Braxton Country Club.

Venue Advice

- **Search for venues in the right location.** Do you want to get married in your hometown, or do you want a destination wedding?

- **Only consider venues that can accommodate your guest count.** You'd be surprised how many venues can only legally seat one hundred, one hundred and fifty, or two hundred guests.

- **When touring venues, figure out what the venue provides and what you need to provide.** Some venues require more rentals than others, increasing the overall expense.

- **Consider a venue that makes the meals in-house instead of relying on a catering company.** This is particularly significant if the quality of food matters to you. Can you imagine paying for steak that has to be cooked hours before the event and transported in to-go boxes?

- **Get a rough estimate of the cost per person after the initial meeting.** The fee for renting out the venue is very different from the cost per person. Some venues require you to hire their kitchen staff or preferred vendors for food, alcohol, or rentals. Preferred vendors can be pricier than sourcing them yourself. It's kind of like going to the movie theatre and being forced to purchase their overpriced refreshments and candy instead of bringing your own.

The Budget Bride

There are plenty of venues that are willing to compromise based on your budget. Be up-front with your budget when reaching out to potential venues. Not all information online is accurate, and the venue may be willing to throw together a custom quote that meets your requirements.

THE DRESS

I've worn stunning white evening gowns, fancier than many women's choice for a wedding gown; it was going to take a lot to impress me. Like a true Southern girl, I discovered pageantry in high school. I won the first pageant I entered, encouraging me to continue competing in the Miss USA and Miss America pageant circuits. In the past, I held the titles of Miss Odyssey (high school beauty queen), Miss Junior Cobb County, Miss Cobb County, Miss Marietta (twice), and Miss Atlanta.

You may be thinking, "Aren't pageants anti-feminist and misogynistic?" or "You were like Honey Boo Boo growing up?" To me, competing in a pageant is feminist. The women I met were strong, smart, and inspiring. Also, I never participated in childhood pageants, so I can't speak on behalf of children who compete.

I met a woman named Mrs. Olivia at my first pageant. She approached me after the competition and asked if I wanted to train with her to prepare for bigger titles. We became very close as she coached me to take home my high school beauty pageant's crown as a junior, which had never been done before.

Mrs. Olivia is one of my idols. To this day, she keeps in impeccable shape, is always glamorous, wears three-inch heels, and wouldn't be caught dead without her long blonde hair in bouncy curls. She has two boys, both adults now, but her house was meticulously kept. She was not the type of mother who let her house become a "boy house."

Mrs. Olivia and I would shop together to select my pageant gowns, and she would always tell me in her sweet Southern accent, "Winners wear white!"

She was correct, winners **do** wear white. Over the years, I've worn the most remarkable white gowns—a beaded white gown, a tulle white gown, an illusion white gown, a mermaid white gown, and so on. Mrs. Olivia's guidance became second nature, and I wasn't going to settle for just any wedding dress. It would need to wow me.

During March and April, Peter and I were living with my parents—how romantic. Our household was under strict quarantine due to my mom's increased risk because of an autoimmune disorder. The only exposure we had to the outside world was when Peter and my dad would endure their weekly grocery store run.

For those who saw the grocery store aisles of 2020, you are well aware of what a competitive sport shopping was. There was no point in making a grocery list because we never knew what meats, fresh vegetables, or paper products would be available. Scoring a four-pack of toilet paper was the highlight of our week. When the men returned from their outing, my mom and I would spend an hour in the kitchen, wearing medical gloves and masks, disinfecting the groceries with Lysol wipes.

After two months of being super vigilant, my mother, grandmother, and maid of honor, Vivienne, broke our quarantine to begin the process of shopping for a wedding dress. Since it takes nine months for a wedding gown to be made, we were anxious to begin the hunt, not knowing how many bridal boutiques we would need to visit before finding **the one.**

I booked my first appointment at Tori's Bridal the day they reopened, albeit with new operating rules, on May 4, 2020. Tori's Bridal is famous for its reality television series that follows the day-to-day events of brides in pursuit of an exceptional wedding gown. I thought this would be a nice place to start after binge-watching several episodes.

When we arrived for our appointment, we were the only customers. The boutique was following a tight, appointment-only schedule to reinforce social distancing. In addition, they were limiting the number of guests brides could bring along.

If I had it my way, I would have brought my entire Italian posse. If you know anything about Italian families, it's probably that we travel as a pack, no matter how big or small the event may be. I had fourteen family members attend my high school graduation when each graduate only received four tickets for the ceremony. Somehow, my mother was able to snag an extra ten tickets. Alas, there would be no way around the guest limit at Tori's Bridal.

Before entering the building, we had to slip on our masks and have our temperatures taken. My mom brought us N95 masks to wear. While they are among the best at keeping out microbes, these were the largest, most uncomfortable masks on the market. It looked like a cereal bowl and covered my entire chin, mouth, and nose, right up to below my eyes. I couldn't breathe well in the mask, probably because of my deviated septum, so I tried to breathe out of my mouth, causing an unpleasant, moist experience.

This was the first time I had left the house in months, and it felt like I was entering a surgical ward. This was **not** how I envisioned my afternoon of wedding dress shopping. Romantic comedies led me to believe that looking for a wedding gown would be fun. There should be music, dancing, all my best friends, and maybe even a bit of bubbly. Despite the harsh light of reality, the four of us were ready to shop until we dropped—which could have been any second after securing the N95 masks across our faces.

We were escorted up to the main floor and introduced to Joe, our dress consultant, who would help us find something. I had a very specific idea of the gown I pictured myself in. I told the ladies, "I want a spaghetti-strapped Aline gown, preferably with an illusion neckline. I don't want anything strapless, because it will be impossible to dance all night. I have never worn a strapless gown that I've liked."

Vivienne and I aimlessly flipped through gowns in plastic bags with no direction. I told Vivienne and Joe, "I want a gown that is slimming but not formfitting." This was essential to me. I wanted to be able to drink as much champagne and eat as many bacon-wrapped appetizers as I wished. More importantly, I wanted to be comfortable, which would not be possible if my gown required Spanx or sticky boobs.

Vivienne pulled four options for me to try on. They were all form-fitting and sexy, the complete opposite of what I asked for. She has a naturally tiny frame and can rock anything skintight, where I feel less self-assured in attire described as slim fit or bodycon.

My dress consultant, Joe, on the other hand, selected four ball gowns. She was influenced by my mom chirping in her ear, "Sara would look like a princess in a ball gown. Can you find some options for her to try on?"

My mom was hard-selling the idea, "This is your last occasion to wear a ball gown!"

I chose two gowns that fit the description of what I was actually looking for.

Joe stood outside the dressing room and announced, "Let me know when you need me to zip you up. I can reach in and try to help, but I'm supposed to maintain a six-foot distance from you at all times."

Do you know how awkward it is to get into a wedding gown on your own? I did my best to situate the gown myself and only asked Joe to adjust it in the back with clips or pins for a better fit.

Wearing a Cinderella-style ball gown, I walked to the elevated runway surrounded by stage lights and mirrors at the center of the room.

My mom and grandmother loved the first gown. "You look like an angel!" they gasped.

"I look like a two-hundred-pound vanilla cupcake!" I replied.

Next, I tried on one of the dresses I picked and headed to the runway. It was an Aline with floral applique, and it resembled gowns I saved on my Pinterest account. When I stood in front of the mirrors wearing the style of gown I'd envisioned wearing for years, I was underwhelmed and disappointed; there was no bling, no inspiration, and no wow factor.

Once again, my mother and grandma blurted, "Oh wow! How beautiful you look!" They were no help at all!

I went back to the dressing room and contemplated which dress to try next. I had eight dresses, and I'd already nixed two of them. The third dress I tried on was one of the gowns my maid of honor selected. It was a formfitting, strapless gown with a long train and overskirt embellished with sequins and rhinestones. This was the exact opposite of what I wanted to wear, but I figured I would humor Vivienne and get it out of the way.

When I saw my reflection in the mirror, I was impressed. It was the first gown I put on that made me feel like myself! This dress was so me! It was dramatic, versatile, and showed just the right amount of skin. It sparkled and wowed. A rush of intuitive certainty overcame me and brought a tear to my eye.

I gushed, "This is it! This is the gown I'll marry Peter in!"

"It's lovely, but don't you want to try on the rest of your options before deciding?" My mother sounded disappointed. "This is only the third gown you've tried on!"

She was right. I needed to at least try on the other options before closing the deal. Appeasing my mother, I tried on the other two ball gowns next. I took the catwalk all frumpy and slouched over. I let the gown wear me instead of me wearing the gown, just to prove my point.

After cycling through the last options, I put my favorite gown on again and immediately came back to life. I stood up taller and looked skinnier. In my eyes, nothing could hold a candle to that gown, and the girls could see that **this** was my gown. We had successfully completed wedding dress shopping in less than an hour, and I was ready to head to lunch. I could not wait to rip off my N95 mask and get something greasy to eat.

I said, "Yes to the Dress!" and spent the rest of the afternoon talking about anything other than wedding dresses. It wasn't until the following morning that my mother had a nervous breakdown.

At 6:30 a.m., my mother charged into my bedroom. "Sara, you only tried on eight gowns! Are you sure you liked that gown? It is not too late to cancel."

I hadn't even had a cup of coffee yet before she continued to question my decision.

"I feel like I couldn't really see what the gown looked like with you wearing a mask, and I couldn't really see over my mask," she insisted. "Maybe we should go back before it's too late."

"Mom, it's fine. It's not that big of a deal. We liked it enough yesterday." I headed toward the kitchen to get a hot cup of coffee before attending a virtual MBA class.

She continued to freak out. "We ordered the gown in ivory, but after researching color swatches, I'm afraid it's going to look yellow on your very pale complexion."

"I am going to have a spray tan when I get married," I reminded her. "So I won't be as pale as I am now." I couldn't believe this was happening.

"The internet says that ivory is better for olive skin and white is better for pale skin. Could we go back to Tori's Bridal and see if they have a white gown you can try on?" My mom continued to push.

This was when I snapped.

"Mom, I made my decision. The gown is going to be stunning. I have so many other selections to make that I don't want to revisit this one. It is final. I have to log into my MBA class now. I really can't talk about this anymore." I stormed out of the kitchen with my coffee.

My mom did anything **but** leave the dress situation alone. By the time I came out of my class at noon, she had managed to track down the designer's phone number and called her.

"I talked to Stacy, the designer of your gown," my mom said. "She was very nice. She's quarantined at her home in Long Island, and she was able to answer my concerns about the ivory-colored gown. She doesn't make gowns white-white because they photograph with a blue hue, but she agreed to make yours in a diamond white."

Within one afternoon, my mom tracked down a highly successful designer and requested a material change on my order. This is the same woman that makes me send emails to her neighborhood Bunco group because she "doesn't know how."

After the letdown of the engagement party, coupled with months of isolation, the shade of my wedding gown meant nothing to me. At the end of the day, I am thankful for my mom's concerns regarding every **tiny** detail.

I waited five months for my dress to arrive, and it was worth the wait. I would need to get over the fact I'd gone with a formfitting, strapless dress that required a pre-wedding diet and Spanx. The moral of the story is to stick to your gut instinct of the type of wedding gown you want. I had valid reasons to stay away from formfitting gowns, even though the style was the only fit to complement my body type.

Wedding Dress Advice

- **Try many styles!** In order to find the best wedding dress for you, be willing to step outside your comfort zone. Try on at least one dress of each style: ballgown, Aline, mermaid, etc. You never know what style you are going to like until you see it on yourself.

- **Buy early.** Most wedding gowns take up to nine months for delivery, and bridesmaid gowns can take as long as four months.

- **Go shopping with a budget in mind.** You don't want to try on the dress of your dreams only to find out it's $3,000 over your budget! It's like tasting a Michelin Star meal but being given Chef Boyardee for dinner—you don't want to compare the two.

- **Bring *blunt* opinions with you!** I once went shopping with a friend of mine who was looking for herself, and her entire audience approved every gown while I shouted, "**next!**"

- **Consider using parts of your mother's gown to create your own!** It wasn't until after I purchased my gown that I tried on my grandmother's vintage tulle gown. I loved it, and I wish I'd tried it on before shopping for my own.

The Budget Bride

You can shop for second-hand wedding gowns online that are in excellent condition. I can almost guarantee it was only worn once! If you don't want to wear a recycled gown, shopping for sample gowns is another great option. Most sample gowns are discounted as much as fifty percent off the original price.

THE SEARCH
FOR A CHURCH

Arranging a Catholic wedding ceremony was one of the most arduous tasks I have ever undertaken, and this is coming from a girl who finds a way to pull off **almost** anything.

Growing up, I never doubted or questioned that I would marry a Catholic or someone who would convert to Catholicism. We would have one of those obnoxiously long Catholic ceremonies complete with a full-length homily and Eucharist.

Even though I grew up in the Bible Belt, nearly everyone I dated was Catholic. In fact, three of my high school boyfriends were Catholic and attended the same church as my family. At the University of Georgia, I could part the red sea (fraternity boys in red football jerseys) and find the one Catholic in a crowd of Baptists.

My Catholic connection comes from my mother's side of the family. Her Italian-Catholic roots stem from New York City and Italy. Everyone in my family was baptized, received their first holy communion, reconciliation, and confirmation in the Catholic church. We take the roles of Godfather and Godmother earnestly, and our faith is strengthened every Sunday afternoon in mass, where my extended family occupies the first two pews. It was only natural to anticipate that the next sacrament I would receive was holy matrimony.

Before I lose you guys, I want to clarify that I am wholly aware of the unpopular opinions of Catholicism. I need to acknowledge its negative history of corruption and pedophilia (which I condemn). But these actions have been perpetuated by individuals and do not speak for all who share this faith. I would not be the one to stray from my family's tradition.

Before the COVID19 pandemic, my life always seemed to fall effortlessly in line. I met my future husband on the first day of graduate school, and barely two weeks later, Peter asked me out on our first official date following a school event. Our MBA program hosted a wine tasting to celebrate our last day of orientation. I agreed to have dinner with Peter under one condition: our classmates could not see us leave together. I was doing everything I could to maintain a professional and competitive edge in front of my new classmates and professors. Peter said it would be a good idea to keep things on the down-low since we had to see each other every day in class, and we didn't want our classmates making any assumptions.

I snuck out of the wine tasting seven minutes before Peter and met him at a restaurant within walking distance. He nailed the first date by scoring an outside table at a French café overlooking the Anacostia River in the Navy Yard. The first thing I noted was Peter's excellent table manners and our ease of conversation. My biggest pet peeve is a man who is rude to waitstaff or chews with his mouth open. We didn't even get our appetizers before I found out that Peter was a confirmed Catholic.

Our worlds were aligning, and by the end of dinner, it was transparent that Peter was the type of man I had been looking for my entire life. He seemed intelligent, hardworking, and placed an emphasis on family and faith. Peter has since proven to be all of those things and more.

When we first got engaged, Peter volunteered to take charge of our preparation for our Catholic wedding ceremony. "I know you are going to have your hands full with the reception," he said. "I can look into finding a church near our venue. I know my mom is going to be happy that we're having a Catholic ceremony because my sister didn't have one, and my brother won't get married in a church either."

I don't think Peter fully understood the colossal commitment he was signing up for.

Thirteen months before our planned wedding date, Peter and my mom began calling every Catholic church between Buckhead and downtown. With our reception in Midtown, we needed a Catholic church no further than a twenty-five-minute drive from our venue. If we settled on a church any further from our venue, we risked logistical issues with the notoriously unpredictable Atlanta traffic.

"I've reached out to fifteen Catholic churches to ask for their availability on May 8, 2021, but I haven't heard back from them," Peter revealed, two weeks into his mission.

"I'm sure their offices are closed because of COVID. Did you leave voicemails?" I asked.

Peter and my mom left multiple voicemails and emails at every church. Weeks went by before they heard back from the Catholic churches within a twenty-five-minute radius from our venue.

"Every Catholic church is booked through the end of June 2021." My mom broke the bad news.

I was shocked to learn this but optimistic that we would find something else.

"Why don't we look into other churches nearby? We can look into Christian churches, Methodist churches, nondenominational churches. Really, anything in Atlanta," I offered.

"It won't count in the eyes of the Catholic church," Peter pointed out.

"Well, we aren't going to push back our date!" I got frustrated.

My mom had an ingenious idea, "Let me call the archdiocese of Atlanta and see what our options are. I am pretty sure a Catholic priest can assist in a ceremony in another church, and it counts."

The same woman who makes me print her UPS return labels because she "doesn't know how" got in contact with the archdiocese of Atlanta and explained our situation. Peter and I would need to complete all premarital counseling through the Catholic church and find a priest willing to assist in a non-Catholic ceremony. If we could do those two things, our marriage would be official in the Catholic church.

I found four non-Catholic churches within a five-minute drive from our venue, and two of them had May 8, 2021, available. Both churches were far more impressive than any Catholic church nearby.

I was slightly disappointed that Peter and I wouldn't have a Catholic ceremony, but I was relieved we wouldn't have to get married at two in the afternoon or seven at night, the only two times the Catholic church allows mass on Saturday. We decided on Grace Christian Church for our ceremony because I was enamored with the old-world gothic cathedral. We were able to schedule our ceremony for five in the evening, which was ideal.

After a month of rejections from Catholic churches, Peter and I were delighted to secure a church. Now, all we had to do was find a Catholic priest to assist in the ceremony and complete our premarital counseling.

Peter called his mom to share the news. "Hey, Mom! We picked a church for the ceremony! It's Grace Christian Church in Midtown."

"I thought you wanted to get married in the Catholic church?" His mother sounded uncertain.

"We do, but we couldn't find a church available on May eighth," Peter explained.

"All of the churches were unavailable? Even the church Sara went to growing up?" she asked doubtfully.

"We only looked at churches within a twenty-five-minute drive of the venue. We didn't want a long drive between the ceremony and reception," Peter did his best to clarify the situation.

"Okay...I just thought you wanted to have a Catholic ceremony. I'm confused. If you want to be Christians when you get married, you don't need my approval," she went on.

Peter tried to catch his mother up to speed with the last month of wedding planning. "Mom, that's not the point. We don't want to convert to another religion. We are going to see if we can get a Catholic priest to assist in the ceremony. We are signing up for premarital counseling through the Catholic church. We're just renting a church that had our date available, that's all."

His mother was not following. "Peter, don't go out of your way to get married Catholic for me. I don't have any say in what religion you practice once you're married."

"Sara and I both want to be married Catholic. It's important to us! We aren't doing it for you. That's not the point. Anyway, it's a really cool church." Peter closed the topic and moved on to other things.

After the call, Peter and I discussed who would take charge of what elements for the ceremony.

"I will coordinate our rehearsal and ceremony with Grace Christian if you focus on getting together the paperwork needed for the premarital counseling through the Catholic church," I said. "I can reach out to a few Catholic priests I know to see if they will assist in the ceremony. All of the premarital counseling will be up to you, okay?"

Peter agreed to hold up his end of the bargain.

In the meantime, I emailed every priest I knew growing up, asking if they were available to **assist** in a wedding ceremony.

To: Father Kyle
From: Sara La Chapelle
Date: June 6, 2020, at 3:56 p.m. EST
Subject: Please consider marrying us!

Hi Father Kyle,

Growing up, I was a member of St. Rita's Catholic Church. I am moving back to Atlanta from Washington, DC, with my fiancé Peter Trelenberg. We are both confirmed Catholics and would love it if you could be a part of our wedding ceremony.

It would mean so much to me to have you assist in this ceremony. Please, please give us a call so we can further discuss our plans for the wedding. It will take place on May 8th, 2021, in the city of Atlanta.

Thank you for your consideration.

Much love,
Sara & Peter

Weeks went by, and I didn't get a single reply. It turned out that Catholic priests don't like being the assistant coach or sous chef of a wedding ceremony, and they definitely don't like performing sacraments in a non-Catholic church.

The lack of correspondence between the Catholic priests forced me to explore other options for the Catholic church to approve our marriage. According to my research, if we couldn't find a Catholic priest to assist in the ceremony, we would have to hold a separate ceremony in a Catholic church before or after our wedding.

Peter was not thrilled with the idea. "If we get married in a private ceremony, we have to do it **after** the wedding. I want our wedding day to feel special."

Peter was right. I didn't want to exchange vows at a private ceremony beforehand. I wanted to be impassioned when we shared our vows for the first time in front of our guests. I scheduled a private ceremony at St. Rita's, the church I grew up in, for the Tuesday following our wedding. It wasn't until November, six months before our wedding, that we heard back from St. Rita's with the next steps in our Catholic ceremony.

Church Search Advice

- **Consider compromising on the church in exchange for location.** Do you mind having a long drive between the ceremony and reception venues? We didn't want guests to spend time commuting between the two, so we chose a church within a five-minute drive from our reception.

- **Opt for a church that offers your ideal ceremony time.** Would you prefer a gap between the ceremony and reception or have your ceremony lead right into the reception? We wanted our ceremony to lead into cocktail hour. In our case, we found a church that held ceremonies at 5:00 p.m. on Saturdays so we could begin cocktail hour immediately following the ceremony.

- **Think about providing transportation from the ceremony to the reception venue.** If you plan on having your ceremony and reception in different locations, look into providing a bus to transport guests between the events. Have the transportation start at your recommended hotel to take guests to the ceremony and then the reception. By starting at a hotel, no one has to leave their car at either venue, and no one will get lost on their way.

THE INVITATIONS

When I first started the wedding planning process, I didn't think twice about the invitations. I've been invited to more weddings than I can count on my fingers and toes, and I have trouble recalling **any** of the invitations.

The mentality I had going into my first stationery meeting was to spend as little money as possible. I'd rather spend the money toward something that would be visible on the day of the wedding (e.g., booze, the band, florals). People will only throw away our invitations after the wedding, and I highly doubted anyone would say, "Sara's wedding was a blast, but her invitations were lame."

I met Heather, the founder of Cotton Lilies, a highly regarded stationery company in Atlanta, one afternoon at her office. I brought my mom, dad, and wedding planner Madison to listen in on the first meeting. No matter what level of quality I landed on, I needed Madison to back up my decision because the price of invitations had skyrocketed since my parents got married almost thirty-eight years ago.

Before the meeting, I filled out the required three-page questionnaire on wedding details, including color scheme, location, date, and wording options. There was even a space to include photographs for inspiration. I had designed my wedding with InDesign (my desktop publishing software) over a month prior and had a seven-page PowerPoint spread with my florals, cake design, colors, and even bridesmaids' dresses. In the space provided, I attached snippets of my wedding design on the questionnaire. I hoped sharing more information up front would make the initial meeting quicker.

For wedding inspiration, go to
www.thecovidbridebysara.com/post/weddinginspo

Heather greeted our crew at the front door of her office and directed us to a cushy lounge with a plush sofa and chairs. After the pleasantries, she carried over two heavy scrapbooks with wedding invitations for us to flip through as inspiration.

"You can pick and choose what you like from different invitation suites." Heather held up a board showcasing an entire suite. "Also, don't get caught up on the colors. We can make your invitations in your blush and gold color scheme."

As I flipped through the collection of invitations, nothing amazed me. Any of the invitation samples would have been more than satisfactory, but there wasn't a single invitation suite I wanted to modify with our details and colors.

In my head, I kept thinking, *just choose something! You don't even care about the invitations. I promised myself I wouldn't fuss over this detail.* Like it always does, my

Leo-dramatic brain took control, and I began throwing out concepts that were floating around in my head.

"I'm envisioning a logo that ties together all of our wedding items. Could we create some sort of crest combining Peter's and my initials?" I asked Heather.

"Yes, I was going to recommend that. From the photos you sent me, your event looks formal. I was thinking we could even use your logo on the invitations, stamps, and wax seal," Heather added.

We were on the right track. I asked myself, *what would Kate Middleton do?* I touched over twelve different papers before choosing a thick, savory cotton. Heather and I continued to work through the ideas I had in my head. Surprisingly, my dad involved himself in the process and agreed with my choices.

We solidified the main details, and I asked Heather to design a weekend itinerary to add to the invitation.

"I've never added a weekend itinerary. Usually, my brides put that information on the website," Heather said.

From my experience, no one ever checks the wedding website, and no one knows what is going on the weekend of the wedding. *I'd rather avoid a thousand questions and provide an itinerary.* I pushed back with, "I know for a fact that my family won't check our wedding website."

Before ending the meeting, Heather summarized our decisions. "Okay, so we want the text to be printed in a mix of charcoal letterpress and gold foil press. At the top of the invitation, we will blind emboss a custom crest that I will design for you. For the envelope, the inside will be a custom watercolor print with white roses, blush peonies, and a touch of garden-style greenery. I will design RSVP cards and a weekend itinerary beginning on Thursday and ending on Sunday with the locations and times. For the wax press, I think the prosecco gold monogram will look the best. Lastly, I will design a matching rehearsal dinner invitation that you can think about later."

"Sounds great. I look forward to seeing your designs," I gushed while packing up my things.

Two weeks later, Heather emailed us a first mockup of the invitation suite and an initial quote. I couldn't believe how much it was going to cost for everything we discussed, but her designs were so elegant that I was willing to spend more toward the invitations than anticipated. I had plenty of money in my budget, but I was still hoping to take up my dad's offer to use leftover funds to purchase the Restoration Hardware sectional couch I had been eyeing for years.

I printed out the invitation proofs and reviewed each page in fine detail. I emailed Heather with a handful of changes. I'd originally listed my parents' address for the RSVP cards, but Madison advised that these be mailed to her. She told me that keeping track of the entrees was part of her job.

Because COVID made things unpredictable, I wanted my invitations sent out a month earlier than the typical timeline. Since it was so grueling keeping track of my guests' address changes, I figured I needed more time to make sure everyone got their invitation.

It was still early in our timeline, but I went ahead and signed off on the final designs.

Wedding Invitation Advice

- **Send the RSVP cards to your home address.** You'll understand why when you get to the chapter "The RSVPS."

- **Provide an online RSVP option on your invite.** If people forget to mail in their responses, this will give you a backup method for accurately counting the RSVPs.

- **Check and then double-check.** When reviewing invite proofs, print a copy and ask for at least two more sets of eyeballs to review them before signing off. If you designed them, you are less likely to catch mistakes.

- **Consider sending an itinerary with your invites.** My weekend itinerary was my guests' favorite part of my invite, despite Heather believing it was unnecessary. My guests were thrilled to receive that information up front!

THE
weekend itinerary

THURSDAY, MAY 6, 2021
5PM - 8PM | WELCOME BBQ
Out-of-town guests & family only

LA CHAPELLE RESIDENCE
Address here
CASUAL DRESS
RSVP: WEDDING@SARALACHAPELLE.COM
(Please include "BBQ" as the subject of your RSVP email.)

FRIDAY, MAY 7, 2021
6PM - 9PM | REHEARSAL DINNER
Invite only

RESTAURANT HERE
Address here
FORMAL DRESS

FRIDAY, MAY 7, 2021
8:30PM - 11 PM | COCKTAIL HOUR
Open to all guests

RESTAURANT HERE
Address here
FORMAL DRESS

SATURDAY, MAY 8, 2021

WEDDING DAY

BLACK TIE

*Transportation will be provided to and from the
ceremony and reception starting from (Hotel) at 4:00pm.*

SUNDAY, MAY 9, 2021

FAMILY BRUNCHES

11 AM | LA CHAPELLE FAMILY BRUNCH

Open to all guests on their way out of town.

LA CHAPELLE RESIDENCE

CASUAL DRESS

RSVP: WEDDING@SARALACHAPELLE.COM

(Please include "Brunch" as the subject of your RSVP email.)

10 AM - 12 PM | TRELENBERG FAMILY BRUNCH

Open to all guests on their way out of town.

HOTEL HERE

ADDRESS HERE

CASUAL DRESS

RSVP: WEDDING@SARALACHAPELLE.COM

(Please include "Brunch" as the subject of your RSVP email.)

FOR MORE DETAILS, PLEASE VISIT:

WWW.OURWEDDINGWEBSITE.COM

The Budget Bride

To get a better price on wedding invitations, design your own or use a template from Minted or another invitation company. If you are set on custom invitations, ask for a pricing sheet for the different paper weights, printing options, and postage to see if you can make adjustments that fit your budget. Consider what invitation components are absolutely essential and what works for your wedding. For example, if RSVP postcards fit your style, they are less expensive than a card with an envelope.

THE REHEARSAL VENUE

A few weeks before our engagement, Peter's father was run off the road while biking and had to be rushed to the hospital for surgery. At the time, family members, even spouses, were not allowed in the hospital for fear of COVID.

With his father's accident, Peter's family found it tough to express their enthusiasm over our big news. Adjusting to pandemic life was distressing enough without the strain of recovering from a life-altering injury. It felt wrong to celebrate our engagement when the world was suffering, Peter's dad was learning to walk again, and he still didn't have a job lined up after graduation.

The rehearsal dinner was only briefly mentioned by my future in-laws. I could sense tension between Peter and his family and promised myself I would not touch the rehearsal dinner with a ten-foot pole. *It's entirely up to Peter's parents to host the rehearsal dinner, and I don't want to overstep their boundaries,* I told myself. *I will do my absolute best to avoid inserting myself in this process.*

Whatever type of event the Trelenbergs wanted to host, I would be more than delighted to attend. It was imperative for me to remain neutral because I did not ask for any involvement from them for the wedding. Although it is an antiquated tradition, my father had offered to cover the wedding expenses, and I wouldn't need to collaborate with his family during the planning process.

By summertime, I began hiring my key vendors. The photographer and videographer sent me a proposal for the rehearsal dinner as well. Even though I promised myself I wouldn't get involved, I couldn't stop myself from sharing the information with Mrs. Trelenberg. I wanted the Trelenbergs to be able to hire a quality photographer or videographer for the rehearsal while a good one was still available.

I emailed Mrs. Trelenberg the two quotes I received for the rehearsal dinner. In the email, I asked if she wanted to reserve the photographer and videographer with a fifty percent down payment.

Mrs. Trelenberg reviewed the quotes and immediately declined the videography contract, stating, "We don't need a photographer and a videographer. It will be overkill." She accepted the quote from Thompson Photo.

I was thankful for her booking a photographer, but I couldn't shake the feeling of rejection when she declined the videography quote. I felt like this was her way of saying, "I am not sure if you and Peter are going to last, and I don't want to spend a fortune on the rehearsal dinner just in case." I knew I was reading too much into it, but I felt a deep insecurity that his family didn't take me seriously.

Based on how Mrs. Trelenberg's trivial choice made me feel, I knew I couldn't involve myself with the rehearsal dinner, or my overthinking, sensitive self would get me in trouble. When I was designing the wedding invitations, the rehearsal dinner came up.

"Would you like us to design matching rehearsal dinner invites?" Heather from Cotton Lilies asked.

Keeping in mind that I'd hired one of the priciest companies in Atlanta, I turned down the offer. "No, thank you. I am going to let Mrs. Trelenberg handle it," I replied, doing my best to avoid the middleman situation.

"It would be more expensive for a separate invitation. We can add the rehearsal dinner and save around four to seven hundred dollars on envelopes and postage depending on the number of invites."

"Oh, I didn't think of that. Sure, go ahead and design a matching invite for us," I muttered, breaking my promise of remaining uninvolved.

Weeks later, I sent the rehearsal dinner proofs to Mrs. Trelenberg, and she called within an hour of receipt. "I got the proofs! I love them; they look amazing!"

"Thank you, they did a nice job," I agreed. "We have time to figure out the location; invitations won't go to print until December."

"Yes, how many people are you inviting?" she asked. "That will influence where we have it."

I hesitated, not wanting to share how many invites I wanted to send. "How many people would you like to have in total?"

"I don't have a number in mind. I know you have a big family. We do, too," Mrs. Trelenberg rattled on. "Just send me a list."

Because I wanted to avoid any miscommunications, I sought final approval before moving forward. "That will be around **Seventy-five** people. Is that okay?"

"Yes, that's fine!" she readily agreed.

Phew! I'd been tentative about telling her how many people we wanted to invite to the rehearsal dinner. Seventy-five guests is larger than some weddings.

I thought I was in the clear and had successfully avoided any further involvement with the rehearsal dinner—until one night in October. Mrs. Trelenberg called to see how Peter and I were feeling. We had come down with COVID simultaneously and were quarantining at my parents' house while they were in Florida.

"We feel okay," Peter sighed. "Neither of us can taste or smell anything. I slept for twelve hours yesterday."

"Well, call me if anything changes," she lectured with worry in her voice. "I've heard of people having a cytokine storm and getting worse after they start to feel better."

"We will be fine," Peter reassured her.

"I'll be passing through Atlanta next week and want to stop and check out some rehearsal dinner venues. I found a couple of options on Google. Have you heard of VOS or The Wine Bar?" she asked.

"Nope," Peter replied.

The phone was on speaker, and I couldn't help asserting my opinion. "I don't think you'd like either of those. The food isn't anything special," I called from across the room. Neither location was rehearsal-dinner worthy.

"I have no idea what I'm looking for. Do you have any suggestions you want to send to me?" Mrs. Trelenberg inquired.

Ugh, why did I say anything? What is wrong with me?

"I can connect you with my wedding planner," I blurted on the spot. "She can help consult for the rehearsal dinner. I have a $2,000 credit for the engagement party that never happened."

There was a moment of silence before Mrs. Trelenberg responded. "You don't have to do that! You can always send me ideas you have."

"No, really! It's not a problem. I couldn't get a refund, so you might as well work with her." I tried to sound reassuring through my raspy COVID voice.

It was settled. To remain neutral, my wedding planner Madison would assist with the rehearsal dinner. I did not want to be the one to offer up restaurants that were not her taste, too exorbitant, or even too cheap.

Madison made appointments with four restaurants for Mrs. Trelenberg to visit on her quick trip to Atlanta. Following the tours, Mrs. Trelenberg sat down with us outside my parents' house, six feet apart.

"I went to see all of the restaurants," she told us. "I only liked 3Kitchen. It's close to the hotel and looked appropriate for a rehearsal dinner."

"I am glad you found something!" I was relieved. We'd cleared this hurdle!

"But there is a catch," she cautioned. "The restaurant has another rehearsal dinner that night at five. I know you wanted the dinner to end early so you could host a cocktail hour for Out-of-town guests afterward, but the only time they can take us is 8:00 p.m."

"Oh man...I think 8:00 p.m. is too late. They won't be able to feed us until nine." I did not want the rehearsal dinner to end late. Since I couldn't invite all our Out-of-town travelers to the rehearsal dinner, I needed to at least see them for a drink before the big day. With a late dinner, the cocktail hour would be absurdly late.

"I don't have any other options. What am I supposed to do?" Her exasperation was clear.

"I just think it would be a long wait between the four o'clock rehearsal at the church and dinner at eight. What will everyone do during the wait?" I asked, in an attempt to help her see reason.

"Yeah, I don't know," she confessed. "3Kitchen is still an option because, right now, I don't have anything else."

"There are so many restaurants in Atlanta," I insisted. "I'm sure we can find something. I'll come up with a list for you."

Mrs. Trelenberg was resistant to looking into different venues. She was leaving town in the morning and wouldn't be able to visit additional restaurants. I knew I had to demonstrate that there were other places she could host our rehearsal dinner. Without wanting to, I got involved in the planning. It was either stay out of the rehearsal dinner or end up going to bed at midnight the night before my wedding. The three things I wanted for my wedding were a good night's sleep, a good hair day, and good weather.

Over the rest of the night, I came up with possible restaurants. I didn't just list any nearby restaurant; I made a list of real contenders. My criteria were proximity to the venue, two to three money signs on Google, private event space or a restaurant buyout option, and firsthand experience. I didn't want to risk including places I had never been before. It would be an overpriced dinner, and I wanted Mrs. Trelenberg to be happy with it.

I sent the list to Mrs. Trelenberg. She contacted my top three choices and booked the one available for May seventh without tasting the food or touring the space. All she knew from me was that it was close to my old apartment in Midtown, and I thought the food was tasty.

After that, I did my best not to re-involve myself in Mrs. Trelenberg's event.

Rehearsal Venue Advice

- **Discuss details ahead of time.** Planning a wedding can be tricky when you are just getting to know your future in-laws. There are no rules that say who should pay for what anymore. Talk with your future spouse about how you want your families to be involved with the wedding process beforehand.

- **Know the difference between overstepping and being helpful—there is a very fine line!** If one side of the family lives in another state and isn't familiar with the wedding location, help them get acquainted with the area. I should have provided a list of restaurants to Peter's family to look into from the start, but I didn't want to overstep.

- **Consider a rehearsal venue that is in close proximity to the rest of your wedding events.** Our rehearsal dinner was within walking distance from our hotel block. This was extra convenient for those traveling from out of town because guests didn't need to rent a car or pay extra cash for Ubers and Lyfts.

The Budget Bride

To save money on the rehearsal dinner, consider inviting the bridal party and close family members only! The moment you invite a second or third cousin to join, the line gets blurry on who should or should not be included. Another way to save money is to host the rehearsal dinner early! The earlier you host the event, fewer people will be inclined to eat and drink. Also, send your rehearsal dinner invite in the same envelope as the wedding invites to save money on envelopes, printing addresses, and postage.

THE FIRST DANCE

In my opinion, the first dance embodies the couple's relationship and is one of the most integral moments for the couple to express their love, unity, and harmony.

I have thought about the first dance so much that I created my own theory that links a couple's personality type with their choice of first dance. My theory is based on complete speculation and may only apply to couples in the South. Peter has told me the first dance is not a big deal on the west coast. As an attendee of multiple weddings, I believe I can assume a lot about a couple based on their first dance.

A couple that tactfully plans and executes their first dance is the same couple that has discussed future children, opened a joint savings account, has a Roth IRA, and has dedicated hours to premarital counseling (religious or otherwise). This couple has a five-year plan and a ten-year goal. The couple with a choreographed dance routine cares about first appearances and wants to present a unified front to the outside world. They love the spotlight and being the center of attention.

Couples who spend minimal time on their first dance (apart from choosing the song) are overall more easygoing. This type of couple would rather let life unfold naturally and seize opportunities as they present themselves. They will make up their rules and would rather spend their free time indulging in other activities they both find amusing.

The non-choreographed couples are probably more fun than the choreographed couples, but as one of the latter, I have to question their laissez-faire attitude. At the end of the day, whether a couple chooses to choreograph their first dance or not, I believe their choice speaks to their courage and creativity.

I was not just **any** theatre nerd growing up; I was a dancer for fifteen years, president of my high school thespians, and a theatre major at the University of Georgia. One of my first paid jobs in high school was choreographing high school musicals, dance routines, cheerleading halftime shows, and pageant opening numbers. It might sound crazy, but I cared more about our first dance than our vows. I know how to put on a spectacular show, and I was not going to let this opportunity slip through my fingertips. Peter's and my first dance would warrant a standing ovation!

Even with fifteen years of dance experience, I didn't want to bank on my ability to choreograph a partner routine without professional help. I needed a dance instructor to guide my ideas and teach Peter how to move. I typed "wedding first dance teachers near me" into a Google search, and a handful of names popped up, but I clicked on the first name and sent Bert an email.

To: Bert Harmony
From: Sara La Chapelle
Date: August 19, 2020, 2:14 p.m. EST
Subject: Wedding Choreography

Hi there Bert,

My name is Sara La Chapelle. I am getting married on May 8th, 2021, with 10 people or 300 people! Either way, I'd like a choreographed dance for my first dance and for the father-daughter dance.

I am located in Peachtree City but can travel to your studio. My fiancé has no dance experience and needs all the help he can get.

Please let me know if you are accepting clients at this time.

Thank you,
Sara La Chapelle

Bert responded the next day. We arranged to meet for our first lesson on August twenty-sixth without a song in mind. We had a solid nine months before our wedding, which gave us plenty of time to meet and take breaks for holidays, travel, jobs, and family obligations. Peter has many redeeming qualities, but unfortunately, rhythm is not one. He was going to need as many lessons as possible before the wedding.

I still remember the day I found out that Peter was musically challenged. I had only known him for two weeks, but he asked me if I could drive him across town to his apartment after class. As much as I didn't want to take an extra thirty minutes out of my day to drive in the complete opposite direction of my apartment, I couldn't say no to his piercing blue eyes. Driving him home became a routine, and on our car rides, I would share new music.

When Peter started vibing with the music, he would snap along, painfully offbeat. I didn't say anything to him the first three times, but finally, on the fourth car ride, I gently caught Peter's snapping hand and blurted, "You know you're offbeat, right?"

That car ride is one of my favorite memories of us from our early days of getting to know each other. Despite Peter's lack of rhythm, I still fell for him. He was almost faultless in every other way, so I could look past the fact that he couldn't spin me around the dance floor.

You know the saying you marry someone like your father? This must be true because closer to the wedding date, I began taking lessons with my dad. If Peter is a five out of ten on the dance floor, my dad is a three. They are both generous, kind, and spirited men with impressively clumsy footwork.

Our first meeting with Bert was more of an interview. I needed to confirm that he was a legitimate instructor and not some serial killer that I emailed my parents' home address to. I would have met him at his dance studio or coffee shop, but because of COVID, neither place was an option.

Before Bert arrived at my parents' house, Peter and I cleared out the basement by rearranging furniture to create an open space for a dance floor. We set up a table in the corner of the basement where we could sit down and chat with Bert before getting started. He was punctual, wearing dark jeans and a black button-down. Peter and I introduced ourselves and briefly told him about how we met and that we were living with my parents until we figured out our next move.

Once acquainted with each other, I got down to business. "We don't have a song picked out yet. I was looking to get your advice. We want something upbeat but still sentimental. Oh, and I'd like to eliminate Frank Sinatra or Ed Sheeran. They're overplayed at weddings."

We were flipping through song ideas when I realized we were going to have to overcome an obstacle—my memories associated with music. I tend to be sensitive and take music and lyrics to heart. Music has always been an obvious way for me to communicate (especially with past boyfriends). Once I connect a song to an emotion or a person, my memory is triggered whenever I hear that song.

Bert was doing his best to suggest possible artists while Peter played snippets of the songs on his phone. For every song, I was having a strong, immediate reaction of **no**.

Despite my negative reaction, Bert kept trying.

"Ray LaMontagne?"

"No."

"John Legend?"

"Nope."

"Adele?" Bert said.

"God, no. I'm sorry, it's a long story."

"Vance Joy?"

I tried not to come off rude. "I love him, but no."

"The Lumineers?" Bert tried again.

"No." I was getting disheartened.

"Ben Howard?"

"Also, a no." I lowered my head into my hands.

Eventually, my mom overheard the conversation and snuck down to the basement to help.

She whipped out her phone and began playing songs on YouTube that **she** thought would be suitable first dance songs. She played slow and sappy country songs that brought tears to my eyes. I don't know if it was because of the music, or if I was so overwhelmed by listening to all of these love songs with emotional triggers.

I couldn't handle it anymore. "Could you please stop playing music? I need to think."

The song came to me. "What about 'Lover' by Taylor Swift and Shawn Mendez?" I turned to Peter and said, "This song has meaning to us." I showed Bert and Peter a video clip from the remake of *Beauty and the Beast* with Emma Watson and expressed how I'd love to incorporate a waltz into our routine.

Peter agreed it was a relevant song and announced, "I just need to learn how to waltz!"

We concluded our first lesson without any dancing but scheduled another hour to begin the following week. For the next several months, Bert and I choreographed the first dance together. I'd show him a move that I liked, and he was able to make it into a partner dance by teaching Peter how to counter step each move. He taught Peter the proper hand placements and how to twirl and dip me.

During our lessons, Peter would get flustered and frustrated with certain steps or forget his moves. We'd take five and try again. It wasn't easy for Peter to put himself out there, and his commitment to learning our first dance was one of the greatest gifts he gave me during this process. We rehearsed for months in my parents' basement until we eventually needed more room to properly execute the routine. Bert made a deal with the owner of a nearby dance studio in Palmetto to let us practice there.

It became a routine to meet on Tuesday evenings at the dance studio. There were many weeks I was burned out from work and wedding planning that I wanted to skip practice. I ignored my urge to cancel class and kept to our schedule because I knew Peter needed the extra time to drill the routine into his muscle memory. I'm not going to lie. Our first dance was a **lot** of effort, but we never gave up.

The months passed by quickly, and it soon became only a few weeks before our big day. One Tuesday in dance class, Peter and I agreed that we would not drink any alcohol on the day of the wedding before our first dance. We didn't want to screw up our dance after putting forth so much effort. When I thought about the wedding day approaching, I was thankful I found a partner who would dedicate the time to our first dance.

First Dance Advice

- **If you're doing a choreographed first dance, give yourself at least four months to plan and prepare.**

It can take weeks to select a song or attend enough lessons to feel assured with your dance. Don't make the mistake of pushing this off if it's important to you. The more you can practice, the more polished you and your partner will look on your wedding day.

- **Practice in your dance shoes.** Instead of wearing my wedding shoes for the first dance, I switched into Bloch character shoes—my goto musical theatre footwear. Obviously, you don't need to wear professional dance shoes, but make sure you dance in the shoes you will be wearing. If you switch shoes for the first dance, make sure the heel height matches your wedding shoe height enough to avoid issues with the hem of your dress.

- **Lean into whatever wedding traditions you care about the most.** For us, we were invested in the first dance, and we put in the hours to make it meaningful. If you love creative drinks, it could be tasting one hundred different signature cocktail blends. It might be preparing a song to sing to your spouse at the reception. It could even be learning to say your vows in another language if your partner's family is from another country.

- **Make it memorable!** Your wedding day provides opportunities for you to express who you are as a couple. Find your unique way of expressing who you are so your guests can get to know you two as a couple.

The Budget Bride

The best part about incorporating a special tradition or performance on your wedding day is that it can be absolutely free. It costs nothing to share your own vows, sing a song, display your own artwork, or put together a curated playlist with your favorite music.

THE CATHOLIC PREP

After weeks of silence from my hometown church, a sweet older woman named Betty reached out to schedule our informational meeting to plan a private Catholic ceremony. We had been emailing St. Rita's church since the beginning of May, and we didn't have our first confirmed appointment for another seven months.

Before attending the first meeting, Peter and I needed to provide original documentation of our holy sacraments to submit to the church. Easy for me, I completed all of my sacraments at St. Rita's and didn't have to contact multiple churches to uncover my paperwork. Peter, on the other hand, had to track down a copy of his baptism certificate from New Jersey, his first holy communion certificate from Houston, and his confirmation certificate from Los Angeles.

The night before our first meeting, I reminded Peter that we couldn't be late. "If we're going to be on time, we need to be in the car by 8:30 a.m. Oh, and wear something nice!"

The next morning, my alarm sounded off at six-thirty, which was just enough time for me to wash, blow-dry, and curl my hair.

I knew I wanted to look my best before meeting the priest who would be the key leader in our Catholic marriage. Once my hair was curled, and makeup applied to my satisfaction, I slipped on a long-sleeve sweater dress and matching over-the-knee suede boots.

Peter waited until the last minute to put on his shoes, brush his teeth, and grab a coat. We didn't leave our apartment until eight-forty, and the later-than-intended departure instantly made me anxious and crabby when our GPS spat out an 8:59 a.m. arrival.

"Step on it!" I ordered. "We can't be the couple that shows up five minutes late!"

Seconds later, Peter and I started bickering like an old married couple.

"You're always late!" I complained.

"Eight fifty-nine is not late!" Peter snapped.

"Oh, is this what our marriage is going to be like?" I scolded. "Are we going to be the family who is always late to Church? Are we going to be the family that makes other people wait because we're late picking up our kids?" I cringed at the sound of my own voice but couldn't stop myself from nagging him.

Our old Volvo sedan sped down the two-lane highway toward the church until we suddenly came to a screeching halt. Sprawled across the highway was a hundred-year-old oak tree that had fallen that night during a thunderstorm. We hadn't anticipated a major detour on our way to the church.

It was almost 9:00 a.m., and by this point, I began to fret. "The only other way to get to the church is if we take Trickery Road all the way around the outskirts of town. It's going to take us another twenty minutes to get there."

Attempting to rescue the situation at hand, I called the office at the church. No one answered. I left a voicemail. "Hi, Betty, It's Sara. Peter and I are on the way. We came across a detour from last night's storm. We will be a little late, but we are still coming!" Simultaneously, I sent an email to her with the same information.

I was cursing my way to church and contemplating turning the car around to avoid the humiliation of walking into the first meeting egregiously late, especially since there were other couples we'd be meeting.

We finally pulled up to the back entrance of the church, and Peter threw the car in park. The two of us bolted toward the front doors only to find that they were locked. We circled the building, testing other entrances. We came across a group of volunteers collecting canned goods.

Out of breath from running in heels, I panted, "Do you happen to know where the Pre-Cana marriage classes are taking place?"

No one knew what we were talking about.

We took another unsuccessful lap around the locked building. Peter and I were just about to give up when a priest popped his head out of the office doors and yelled out, "Sara, Peter? Is that you?"

We ran into the classroom to meet two other couples who had been on time with Starbucks coffees and notepads in hand. It was apparent the couples had been waiting on our arrival. Mortified but now uncomfortable, I quietly mumbled, "Would you mind if I ran to the restroom?" further delaying the start of class.

The rest of the morning was devoted to taking a one-hundred-fifty-question multiple-choice test about our relationship. It covered problem-solving, family planning, financial planning, family traditions, and other significant topics. The priest announced, "You will receive your scores in a few weeks at a follow-up session to discuss the topics you need to address as a couple."

The rest of the session was information overload. The multiple-choice exam was a cakewalk compared to filling out the marriage paperwork and receiving a spiral workbook called *For Better & For Ever: A Resource for Couples Preparing for Christian Marriage*, a paperback book of gospel readings that pertained to marriage, and a booklet with information on the next steps for our Catholic ceremony. As Peter promised, he took ownership of the packet of information and affirmed that he would schedule our next meeting at St. Rita's.

On Monday, December fourteenth (still plenty of time before the wedding), Peter and I went back to St. Rita's to meet with our priest to go over relationship compatibility results. It was a cold evening, and it had been a long day of work for me and a long day of job hunting for Peter. When we arrived at the church, we were introduced to a new priest we hadn't met before.

"Nice to meet you, Father Michael," I chirped. "We're excited to go over our test results!"

"Sara and I have been working through every chapter of *For Better & For Ever*," Peter added, proud of the fact we'd almost completed the two-hundred-page workbook. Peter and I were anxious to hear the results from our compatibility test and willing to put in the necessary effort to strengthen aspects of our relationship that needed help.

Instead of getting the therapy and counseling we expected, the evening took a bizarre turn when Father Michael began telling stories about his childhood and the odd relationship he had with his father. Peter and I sat through the two-hour meeting and hid our yawns underneath our N95 masks. If this was the last thing we needed to do as a couple to be married in the Catholic church, we could get through it!

The evening came to an end around 8:30 p.m. We crashed through the church doors like two kids on the last day of school before summer break. We had completed the steps to be married Catholic, and we were proud! Or so we thought.

It wouldn't be for another few months that we would find out we were not yet approved to wed in the Catholic church.

THE HONEYMOON PLANS

Landing on a honeymoon destination was not going to be a breeze. Growing up, Peter traveled all over the world with his family. When they relocated to Hong Kong to follow his father's career, they began traveling to exotic locations I never imagined were possible outside of movies and *Condé Nast Traveler*.

On one of our first dates, I asked Peter, "What is your favorite destination you have traveled to?"

He shot back with, "Oh—that's a tough question. Probably the Maldives or Mauritius."

"Mauritius?" I questioned, Googling it after the date.

Over the Thanksgiving holiday, I sat down with his sister Emily over a morning cup of coffee and asked her the same question. Emily responded with, "I loved our family trip to Bali, but I also really loved Singapore!" Then she added, "Mike and I went to TelaViv for our babymoon, and that was amazing!"

I questioned Peter and Emily, "What was it like to travel on fourteen-hour flights as children? How did your parents manage to keep a five-, eight-, and ten-year-old calm?"

"We were good kids." Peter shrugged. "We would either sleep, read books, or play with puzzles."

I challenged this response and asked his mother the same question. She confirmed that her children were no problem to travel with and didn't cause any issues. The Trelenbergs love to travel and have fond memories from their idyllic family vacations.

On the other end of the spectrum is my family. The most exotic destination we have traveled to as a family is the Florida panhandle. If my parents couldn't pack it up in our oversized Chevy Suburban and drive it there, the trip wasn't going to happen.

We managed to make it to Busch Gardens and Dollywood as a young family, but that's because both were within a six-hour drive from our house with plenty of Waffle Houses along the route for lunch. Seriously, my mom would only eat lunch if there was a Waffle House, because IHOP, Waffle King, and Cracker Barrel were not sufficient.

Our car rides were anything **but** peaceful, and I can guarantee we did not sleep, read books, or play puzzles like the Trelenbergs. Instead, I'd require the car's undivided attention as I sang my heart out to Celine Dion or the Spice Girls and get mad if anyone talked or tried to sing along with me. When I didn't have the car captive with my subpar vocal performances, my brothers would argue in the backseat over trivial matters.

Just to annoy my dad, my oldest brother, Rob, would blast Eminem on his Sony portable CD player loud enough for the entire car to hear. When my dad couldn't take it anymore, he would reach back, snag Rob's CD player, and throw it out the window.

Rob, TJ, and I loved to play Sweet or Sour, waving at people in other cars to see who would wave back. Looking back, we most likely appeared like stolen children desperately waving for help because my dad would inevitably get pulled over and let off with a warning.

My absolute favorite memory with my brothers was our drive to Disneyworld in Orlando, Florida. Rob and TJ mooned passersby on the highway from the back of the truck. It was all fun and games until Rob got sick and shit his pants.

As you can see, Peter and I have very different experiences surrounding family vacations.

One evening, Peter and I sat down to make a list of possible destinations for our honeymoon. Ideally, we wanted to choose a destination that neither of us had visited before. Our final list of options was sparse because Peter had already traveled to many highly regarded destinations for honeymooners.

Before this exercise, Peter had his heart set on Greece. I couldn't reconcile our honeymoon with the fact that he visited Greece with the high school girlfriend he was intimate with. Nothing turned me off quite like hearing him reminisce about rediscovering Greece, knowing his eighteen-year-old self was on cloud nine during the summer of his international sex-capades.

I read off the list of remaining countries. "Neither of us has visited Ireland, Turkey, Norway, Sweden, Croatia, or Japan."

Unimpressed by our options, we opened up the list to places that Peter had visited before.

"I'll go to Greece as long as we visit someplace else afterward. What about Malta, Corsica, or even a week in Croatia?" I proposed the idea of a two-week honeymoon.

Peter and I agreed to travel to Croatia and Greece. Croatia was accepting tourism at the time, so we went ahead and made our reservations. We would book Greece a couple of months before the trip; we thought there was no way Greece would still be closed after a year of restricted entry.

We were ecstatic with our choice. I romanticize Europe and believe it is full of hidden gems and some of the world's best food. In Europe, you can spend hours making a list of highly regarded points of interest but end up talking to a local who sends you to a nondescript restaurant with the most delicious food you've ever tasted or sends you down a street with exquisite views of the city. Greece and Croatia satisfied my love for art, culture, and cuisine, and Peter's love for the beach and relaxation.

The first thing we did was look into flights. Since Peter was studying for the bar exam and didn't have a job at the time, I agreed to cover the flights with my saved miles and use my credit card during the trip.

I burned an hour on the phone booking two first-class flights to Croatia and used every last Delta SkyMiles point I had collected over the past two years. I looked to Peter to book the honeymoon reservations because, historically, the woman plans the wedding, and the man plans the honeymoon.

Planning is not Peter's strong suit, but he took days investigating the most beautiful cities to visit in Croatia, the nicest hotels, award-winning restaurants, and the best day trips. He put together an intricate itinerary starting in Zagreb. We'd drive down the coast of Croatia in a rental car, stopping in a different city each day and eventually ending in Split. Peter went ahead and reserved luxury sleeping accommodations with five-star reviews. Everything was going to be flawless, and I couldn't wait to go on a long-overdue adventure with Peter.

Three months before our wedding, travel restrictions were updated worldwide. Croatia, the one EU country that had been open to US tourists, changed its travel policy. After all this effort, we would not be able to travel to Croatia after all.

We canceled our reservations and decided to hold off on booking another destination because we didn't want to have to cancel again.

On every step of planning our wedding, I have learned something new. Obviously, not everyone is fortunate enough to travel internationally (or at all) for their honeymoon, and we were blessed to have it as an option, at least in theory.

I wasn't upset because I couldn't travel to Croatia or Greece; I **was** disappointed to miss an opportunity to see the world with Peter at this stage of our lives. We didn't meet in college like our parents, and we didn't have the option to be young and free for a while. We didn't get to grow up with each other, building our lives together along the way. Rather, Peter and I met later in life, and after our wedding, our lives only became busier and more complicated. We have worked intentionally to merge the lives of two independent people, and I'm the happiest I have ever been. When I look back at my younger self who would pack a suitcase the second things became routine, I don't recognize her anymore. I can still remember the deep sadness I felt and my need to stay in motion to avoid coping with heartbreak or reality. I was lost, trying to find my way in the world. With Peter, I have found joy in our routine, yet sometimes boring, life.

Honeymoon Planning Advice

- **Examine your emotions.** Our engagement year was our chance to travel before officially settling down. The emotions I had around canceling our travel plans highlighted my fear of growing up. I'm here to share with you that **it is okay if you are scared of getting older, settling down, and falling into a routine with someone.** Just because you are getting married doesn't mean you don't still wish for crazy trips around the world with fewer responsibilities. I do believe you will find joy in your new routine, just as I found it in mine, even if you celebrate the little wins, like a new vacuum.

- **It's worth the wait.** If you can't visit the destination of your dreams due to travel restrictions, finances, or other obligations, wait before booking just anything. You can take a mini-moon right after the wedding for a few days and take a longer trip later.

The Budget Bride

Sign up for a credit card with travel rewards! If it weren't for my Delta SkyMiles credit card, I wouldn't have been able to afford the airfare. If you have the flexibility, book your flight on a less busy travel day like a Wednesday or Saturday to save extra cash. Depending on where you are traveling, staying in an Airbnb may be a cheaper option, while other times it can be more costly than a hotel. Make sure to cross check the prices for sleeping accommodations.

THE
STATIONERY ITEMS

Stationery is an essential part of every wedding. Most often, these items serve a practical purpose, such as a ceremony program or dinner menu. Stationers have moved beyond just paper products and now carry a variety of keepsakes as well. Today, brides can personalize just about anything, from napkins to custom drink coasters!

Cotton Lilies, our invitation vendor, offered additional services and personal touches for our wedding. I worked with Heather, the founder and principal designer. At the time, I still had a healthy budget remaining for stationery, and I was antsy to discuss the next steps.

In meeting with Heather, we dreamt up all sorts of stationery possibilities. We nailed down design ideas for nonnegotiable items like the ceremony program, escort cards, and dinner menu. After that, we designed a letter for welcome gifts and a tag for our party favors—"Cheers to Forever." We even brainstormed ideas for a bar sign for my signature cocktail called

The Rosie, a gorgeous rose-colored cocktail named after my dog. I met with the lead mixologist at my venue to craft this refreshing drink made with gin, tonic water, fresh lime juice, cranberries, and edible flowers. Heather would design a sign with a watercolor painting of Rosie's face and quote me for four, one to place at each bar.

We didn't stop there. We discussed custom signage for every aspect of the ceremony and reception. We talked about a welcome sign, a massive portrait from our engagement, reserved signs for ceremony seats, a guest book sign, table numbers, and bar menu signs. Lastly, we talked about white and gold S&P monogrammed cocktail napkins, cocktail stirrers, and gold boxes of matches.

"I think we have enough items for now! When will I get these designs?" I said, ready to end the hour-long meeting with Heather.

"I prefer to order everything about one month before the wedding. A lot can change in six months," Heather replied.

"That makes sense. Could we go ahead and order the welcome bag letter and the party favor tags?" I asked. "I'd like to start those projects sooner rather than later."

"Sure. We will revisit everything else in April when you have your RSVPs for the escort cards," Heather added.

As much as I hated putting off the design process for these treasures, I didn't argue with her. In hindsight, Heather was right to wait to design anything because **everything** ended up changing.

The Budget Bride

The most economical way to add stationery accessories to your wedding is by creating them yourself! Websites like Etsy offer custom napkins and welcome sign templates that you can modify on your own at a fraction of the expense compared to using a stationery vendor. Also, you can print just about anything from FedEx. For my friend's engagement party, I printed a twenty-four- by thirty-four-inch canvas of their engagement photo for only sixty-four dollars!

For photos, go to
www.thecovidbridebysara.com/post/stationery

THE WELCOME GIFT

While nailing down our wedding vendors, a venue, and the church ceremony, my mom and I started on some of the smaller details we could handle on our own. The first task was a welcome gift for our Out-of-town guests. With more than half of our guests traveling to Atlanta to celebrate our special day, it felt imperative to assemble a gift to give them upon their arrival at the hotel.

I had already procured a room block at the NOVA Hotel, located five minutes away from our venue. I was able to snag a reasonable rate of $175 a night for my wedding weekend, which was unheard of for a four-star hotel in Atlanta. Before moving forward with our welcome gifts, I wanted to confirm that the hotel staff would be able to distribute our gifts. The lead coordinator for events reassured me that it would not be a problem. Scanning our initial guest list, I estimated Seventy-five welcome bags would be needed.

I wanted to put together a gift our guests would appreciate. For the most part, brides assemble welcome bags with random snacks with little rhyme or reason to their choices. Since I hadn't met any of Peter's friends yet, I would use this small window to showcase our personalities. As an individual, I can come off as high maintenance and high energy. But as a couple, Peter and I are mannered yet authentic. We clean up nicely, but we are unsophisticated at times. I wanted our welcome bags to be filled with our favorite gas station snacks to portray our approachable temperament.

I drafted a welcome letter to our guests and emailed Heather from Cotton Lilies to design it to match our wedding invitations.

Dear family and friends,

Welcome to Atlanta, Georgia. The home of the Atlanta Braves, peaches, peanuts, Southern belles, and traffic. Our engagement year has been a whirlwind, and we can't believe that our wedding weekend is finally here. It means the world to us that you have taken the time to celebrate the joining of our families.

You are here this weekend because you are an important part of our lives, and we are eternally grateful for your love and encouragement.

Much love,
Sara & Peter

Inside the welcome bags is where the fun began. The back of the letter read:

We have put together a box of our favorite things to get your weekend started.

Sara's Favorite Snacks
Voodoo Chips & Beef Jerky
Peter's Favorite Snacks
Cheez-Its & Sour Patch Kids
Sara's Favorite Beverage
Pellegrino
Peter's Hangover Cure
Pedialyte & Fiji Bottled Water

It took my mom and me two months to complete this relatively simple task. While we were waiting for our welcome gift letters and tags, I went ahead and ordered white glossy gift bags, blush tissue paper, and all the snacks. Buying the snack items in bulk was time-intensive during the height of the pandemic because so many companies had shut down production to stop the spread of COVID in their factories.

The welcome letter had already gone to print when I realized I couldn't order enough Voodoo Chips online, so I ended up driving to local gas stations around town and buying the last of their stock. Shopping for snacks was painless compared to cutting Seventy-five thin blush ribbons, hole-punching each monogram gift tag, and assembling the final product.

Each day, my mom and I would go upstairs to the wedding workshop and spend an hour adding one new item to each bag, beginning with the tissue paper on the bottom and moving through the list of snacks. The final product was exactly what I had in mind; the gifts looked classy, though the snacks inside were anything but.

My mom and I finished this task and lined up all Seventy-five welcome gifts across the floor of the wedding workshop for storage until the wedding weekend. We were thankful to complete this one tiny task before moving on to the next one.

We had no idea that more than half of our guests wouldn't receive their welcome gift.

Welcome Gift Advice

- **Don't spend a fortune on a welcome gift for your guests.** You can spend as much as you'd like, of course, but the personalized elements will matter the most. At the very least, write a letter that the hotel can give to your guests with their hotel key.

- **Use the welcome gift to show you appreciate your guests.** Your guests are going out of their way to spend time and money to celebrate you. However, your wedding weekend is going to be too busy to truly connect with each guest. A small token of appreciation will leave a big impact.

- **Provide a list of nearby recommendations.** Along with your welcome letter or gift, you can provide a list of restaurants, bars, salons, and other entertainment in the area that you have personally vetted for guests to explore.

The Budget Bride

A home-printed welcome letter won't break the bank, and it will let your out-of-town guests know you appreciate their effort to attend your wedding weekend. It's only sixteen dollars for one hundred sheets of high-quality cotton resume paper.

For photos, go to
www.thecovidbridebysara.com/post/welcomegift

THE PARTY FAVOR

Wedding guests often overlook the details. This includes subtle touches like party favors, a custom guest book, or a photo gallery of the couple. It's nearly impossible to appreciate all of the little details in the moment because they are too minute to notice on their own. In my eyes, no detail was too small to neglect.

After spending months completing the welcome gifts, my mom and I moved on to conquer the next item on our list—the party favors.

The sky's the limit for party favors. I've gotten custom koozies, monogrammed baseball hats, Jordan almonds (an Italian goto), and even a Chick-fil-A chicken sandwich! Out of all of the party favors I've received, the chicken sandwich was my favorite. I didn't love this party favor because I **love** Chick-fil-A. *Seriously, if the South had an immigration exam, the first question would be, "Do you love Chick-fil-A?" and the second question would be, "What church do you intend on joining?"* I loved it because it represented the couple's casual and wholesome personality.

When it came time to plan my wedding, I didn't have to contemplate what type of party favor I would offer my guests. Since college, my Pinterest board would attest that I'd leave my last and final impression with a bottle of wine.

Growing up with a French last name, I took an interest in all things French: wine, artisanal cheese, and *joie de vivre* (the things in life that make you happy). I'd like to imagine that wine represents my personality—powerful yet refined, with a subtle sweetness. Before charging forward, I ran the idea by Peter. Without a doubt, he loved it.

I began thinking to myself about how best to proceed. *Should we gift mini or full-sized bottles? Full-size bottles would be harder to take home. It will be even more bothersome for guests traveling by airplane. Mini bottles would be less pricy and probably wouldn't be left behind at the hotel. Mini bottles it is! But how many will we need?*

I ran through the numbers. *We mailed three hundred and twenty-five save-the-date cards and can expect that two hundred to two hundred and fifty guests will say yes. Well...maybe less with COVID. If every couple takes home one bottle, we'll need one hundred and twenty-five of them...but what about the single people? They need their own.* I decided we should round up and purchase one hundred and fifty mini bottles of wine.

I began perusing the internet for sparkling wines available in a mini bottle. At this time, stores in the US were rationing bottled water and toilet paper. Other essential items were missing from the shelves, **especially** the wine. People were drinking more wine than ever before, and retailers couldn't replenish their inventory fast enough. For us, this meant that wines and other specialty cargo traveling from Europe were a rarity and marginally higher-priced, including my favorite Italian apéritif, Aperol, and parmesan cheese. I only make light of the situation because the lack of luxury goods was a tiny inconvenience compared to the economic and health crisis sweeping the globe.

With fifty percent fewer shipments of wine coming from Italy, France, and Spain, my options were limited. I spent more time than I'd like to admit calling wine distributors and Wine Warehouse to check on inventory and shipment schedules. The Prosecco, Champagne, and Cava available were brands I had never tasted before, and it was crucial to taste the options before committing.

Before COVID, finding a mini bottle of wine would have been a breeze. I was able to find over twenty different mini bottle brands, but only three wines were available in the quantity I needed within a sixty-mile radius. Being able to track down three options felt like a miracle, and I knew I needed to act quickly before someone else scooped them up.

That afternoon, I drove forty-five minutes to Wine Warehouse in the next town over. I purchased full-size bottles of wines with sufficient quantities of mini bottles in stock. I invited my parents, brother, and Peter to a wine tasting at my parents' house that evening.

I requested my family participate in a blind taste test of the wines and then vote on which bottle was the most attractive. Before dinner, I set the table with three labeled champagne glasses for each person, filled them with wine, and provided a piece of paper and pen.

I gathered my family at the table and outlined the rules. "In front of you are three different sparkling wines. I want you to taste the wines and then rank them one to three, with one as your favorite and three as your least favorite. Try not to say anything out loud when you taste the wines so you don't skew anyone's opinion."

After I collected the votes, I brought the bottles of champagne to the table and asked everyone to tell me which bottle was their favorite.

"I love the gold bottle! It looks so fancy," my mom blurted. "It even matches your colors."

"That's my favorite, too," my brother chimed in.

Peter and my dad did not have a preference, so they agreed with the existing opinions.

Looking at their sheets of paper with the votes, I exclaimed, "Wow, you like the taste **and** the look of the gold bottle! Want to hear the wine details?"

"Sure." My dad played along with my sommelier game.

Pointing to the gold bottle, I announced, "This wine is more fruity than dry. It is filled with soft peach and nut flavors. Isn't that appropriate for Georgia? It is briny and fresh with a soft floral tone of white lilies."

That night, we polished off the remaining wine and ordered one hundred and fifty mini bottles of our Cava brut. The next day, Peter retrieved the heavy cases of wine and brought them to the wedding workshop at my parents' house. To turn these bottles of wine into finished party favors, I worked with Cotton Lilies to design a "Cheers to Forever" tag for each bottle.

Cotton Lilies forgot to hole-punch the tags, so I recruited my mom and grandma. We took up our well-known positions in the assembly line. My grandma cut one hundred and fifty blush ribbons, I punched holes in the "Cheers to Forever" tags, and my mom tied each tag on the bottles uniformly, singeing the ends with a lighter to avoid fraying.

For photos, go to
www.thecovidbridebysara.com/post/favor

Party Favor Advice

- **Find a party favor that depicts you as a couple!** Mini wine bottles were the perfect party favor for us, but that doesn't mean gifting a bottle of wine is suitable for you.

- **Stay within your budget.** More expensive doesn't necessarily mean better. You can spend one dollar per favor or one hundred dollars per favor and still leave a lasting impression. Personally, I prefer gifts that can be thrown away after consumption because I hate holding on to trinkets.

- **Get creative with your party favors!** Some of my favorite party favor ideas include a candle with your own custom logo and scent, a bag of M&M's with your wedding date printed on the candies, or a packet of flower seeds for your guests to plant.

The Budget Bride

Opting for candy or chocolate is a cost-effective party favor. Another reasonably priced item would be a personalized box of matches. Remember, party favors are not mandatory, so if your remaining budget doesn't allow for something you can get enthused about, skip it! Use the remaining funds toward enhancing the aspects of the wedding you care most about.

THE
BACHELORETTE PARTY

What comes to mind when you think of a bachelorette party? I tend to think of warm tequila shots, matching Etsy t-shirts, penis shaped straws, and a bad case of the Sunday scaries. I had a very different idea of what my bachelorette weekend would look like. I visualized more of a glam weekend with my twelve bridesmaids, engaging in daytime activities, spa appointments, and sipping bubbly on a boat.

Bachelorette parties have a bad rep for being exorbitant and inconvenient, so when planning my weekend, I wanted to make sure my girlfriends wouldn't feel financially burdened. I'm not the type of girl who would say, "It's my bachelorette party, and everyone else can fall in line." If that were the case, I would have booked my bachelorette party in St. Lucia and my wedding in the south of France, but I'd never expect my family and girlfriends to dish out the miles and cash for my nuptials.

It's not uncommon for a bride to host a weekend that will cost her girlfriends upwards of $1,000 to $2,000. I know what you're thinking—that's insane, but let me show you the numbers.

For a weekend at a tropical, yet domestic beach, you need to factor in the expense of airfare, transportation, hotel, food, and a gift for the bride.

Take a simple two-night stay in Miami (Friday–Sunday), for example:

- A flight from Atlanta to Miami runs $250–$500 depending on the time of year.

- Budget $300 per person for the hotel, assuming bridesmaids are splitting the expense.

- Budget another $100 for an Uber to and from the airport.

- Set aside another $50 for transportation to and from restaurants and bars.

- Add another $100 per day for food and alcohol (this is a conservative estimate).

- Last, set aside $50 for a small gift for the bride (typically lingerie).

Right there, the charges for this hypothetical two-night stay in Miami is a **minimum** of $1,050.

Let's dig a little deeper. One hundred dollars per day for food and alcohol is a low-ball estimate because of this common scenario. When a group of girls (usually eight or more) in little black dresses with their ringleader wearing white arrive at a restaurant, the waitstaff is immediately terrified.

Upon seating the group, the staff will say something along the lines of, "How are we going to be paying tonight?" or, "I can only split the check two ways," or, "Are we okay with one check?" to avoid the nightmare of splitting the check amongst a table of intoxicated women.

"Stacy and I split the steak."

"I only had one margarita."

"Us four split the appetizers. Can you divide up the calamari four ways?"

"I had the salad, but I said dressing on the side. Can you remove it from my bill?"

In response to the question on how best to divide the bill, there is always one bridesmaid that speaks up and says, "One check is fine," meaning that the table will find a way to split the bill, usually dividing it equally. This is my least favorite tradition because I always end up paying for more than what I ordered. Half of the table orders decadent seafood platters, filet mignons, and multiple martinis, while the other half of the table is too inebriated to order anything other than a soup and water. But when the bill comes, everyone is obligated to throw in a credit card, whether they ordered $20 or $200 worth of food.

It was my goal to hold an inexpensive and convenient bachelorette weekend free of hidden charges. I wanted my bridesmaids to feel appreciated, not resentful, when they checked their bank statements after the weekend.

Once Peter asked for my father's blessing, Vivienne, my maid of honor, and I concocted the ultimate bachelorette weekend itinerary to take place at my parents' house in Palm Beach, Florida, the following January. The girls would arrive at the Palm Beach airport on Friday, and I would have a bus waiting for them. I'd coordinate flights to make sure they all arrived within the same hour.

When my bridesmaids arrived, I would have gift bags, cocktails, and lunch waiting for them. We'd spend the afternoon outside by my parents' pool. For dinner, we'd take a couple golf carts a few minutes down the road to an Italian restaurant.

On Saturday, I would arrange a private pickleball lesson, followed by a tournament. Pickleball is similar to tennis but easier, so anyone can enjoy the game with or without athletic ability. The winners of the tournament would get an hour-long massage with the bride on Monday. Later that day, we would head to the beach bar for lunch and sunbathing. Saturday night would be the lingerie shower. I'd ask my bridesmaids to get me lingerie that represents their personality, and I'd guess who got it for me. If I was right, they would drink, but if I was wrong, I would have to drink! I'd have other fun games to play before dinner.

Sunday morning we'd head out to Miami on my parents' boat. We'd spend the day cruising to Miami and explore South Beach for lunch. Sunday night would be a relaxed pizza party after a long day in the sun.

Monday morning would conclude the trip. The winners of the pickleball tournament would come with me to the spa to get massages. The girls could go paddle boarding, sailing, or kayaking before the bus brought everyone back to the airport.

It would be a jam-packed weekend of fun. My parents generously offered to cover the cost of transportation, lunches, dinners, the beach bar tab, the pickleball tournament, winners' massages, extra hotel rooms, and the boat ride to Miami.

I solidified the bachelorette itinerary four months before Peter and I got engaged. Once engaged in April, I began assembling a PowerPoint presentation of design ideas and completed it by the end of summer. I wanted to give myself time to order everything I was going to need.

For the bachelorette party plans, go to
www.thecovidbridebysara.com/post/bachplans

I envisioned pink balloon arches, streamers, and garlands everywhere. I would have Instagrammable pool rafts, frozen rosé popsicles, custom pink sugar cookies with my name on them, tropical fruit plates, charcuterie boards, a fridge stocked with the best wines and day-drinking favorites, and overflowing vases of pink roses spread throughout the house.

For a gift for my bridesmaid attendees, I shopped around and found custom beach bags, pink and white striped beach towels, pink sunnies, pink reusable straws, monogrammed silk pink PJs, and captain's hats. I spent late nights purchasing the decorations and gifts I needed to execute my vision. I emailed my bridesmaids a PDF itinerary with an hour-by-hour schedule for the weekend, complete with photos for inspiration and a dress code to prepare for the trip.

Given the state of the pandemic, I did request the girls get a COVID test within three days prior to departure for the safety of everyone. I made a point to book extra hotel rooms in addition to my parent's house, just so no one would have to share a bed, but we'd still be spending a lot of time in close quarters.

Two weeks before my bachelorette party, I had all twelve bridesmaids confirmed for the trip. I packed three large suitcases of bachelorette party items and stored them in the wedding workshop until it was time to transport them to Palm Beach.

Fortunately, my job allowed me to work remotely, so I flew to Palm Beach to prepare eight days before my bachelorette weekend. I cleaned my parents' house and took multiple trips to the one and only grocery store forty-five minutes away to stock up on wine, beer, and booze. Vivienne arranged to arrive two days beforehand to help purchase the last of the fresh food, assemble gifts, blow up balloon arches and pool rafts, and decorate every inch of the house and boat.

One week before the bachelorette party, my phone started ringing off the hook with my bridesmaids backing out of the weekend they had committed to more than ten months prior. The worst part about the excuses was that they were valid and justified.

Amelia was the first to call. "Hey, Sara, I'm really sorry to do this, but as you know, my mother passed away ten days ago, and I'm not really in the party mood. I hope you understand."

Carmen was next. "Please don't hate me, but I don't think I can come this weekend. I'm apprehensive about traveling because of my autoimmune disorder. We were traveling this past weekend, and my boyfriend got COVID, so it made me realize how risky I had been. I'm really sorry! I'm on the list to get the vaccine as soon as it's available."

Then Tiffany reached out. "Hey, I'm sorry to do this, but I can't leave DC after the capital was stormed this week. My job really needs me here."

"I'm concerned with the spike in COVID cases and the new strain going around in Florida," Arya explained. "I'm going to have to pass on this weekend. I'm not going anywhere until I get a vaccine."

"I don't think I can travel to Palm Beach from California at the moment," Mia told me. "California just mandated a fourteen-day quarantine for those who leave the state. I wouldn't be able to go back to work for two weeks if I leave. I'm sorry to disappoint you."

"I'm in the hospital right now about to go in for an emergency surgery to get my gallbladder removed. I keep asking the surgeon if I will be able to travel this weekend, and he won't give me a solid answer," Kristen informed me. "I'll let you know ASAP, but I am going to do everything in my power to be there!"

I was less than a week out from my bachelorette party, and my party of twelve had quickly dwindled to a party of six. This was a big weekend for me. It was my way of acknowledging how significant their friendships were to me. I was looking forward to introducing everyone for the first time and seeing how twelve girls from different stages of my life could come together and bond before the wedding.

I panicked and began texting other girlfriends of mine to see if they were available for a last-minute trip. I had dropped a fortune purchasing decorations, gifts, and stocking the house with goodies. Plus, I already prepaid for transportation, extra golf carts, and hotel rooms. I was **not** going to let any of it go to waste.

Trust me, I felt so tacky texting my friends last minute before the trip because it looked like they were the last pick in the NFL draft. Technically, they were my second choice because I couldn't afford to host twenty of my best girlfriends for the weekend.

The stars aligned, and I was able to replace the last-minute dropouts with friends who were available. I was thrilled that my other friends could join the bachelorette weekend as honorary bridesmaids. Everything was back on track after a few phone calls and a last-minute trip to Homestead to track down a seamstress who would change the monograms on the silk PJs I prepared for gifts.

At the end of the day, you can't be upset with your friends if they can't celebrate your bachelorette party. Life has a way of being unpredictable, and it's okay if something else takes precedence over day drinking on a boat. My weekend ended up being a riot. My girlfriends got along with one another and formed new friendships. I even ended up with a new bridesmaid! Oh, and everyone loved pickleball!

Bachelorette Party Advice

- **Plan, plan, plan!** Challenge yourself to think about your bridesmaids when planning your bachelorette weekend.

- **Consider your budget as well as theirs.** Talk to the girls and find out their preferred budget so you don't put anyone in an uneasy situation. If you really want to do an activity and your friends can't afford it, consider covering the expense yourself.

- **Make an itinerary for the weekend!** When you are coordinating with a large group of women, it's best to have set plans. It's no problem to cancel a dinner reservation last minute, but it's nearly impossible to book a table for twelve an hour beforehand.

- **Include a dress code on the itinerary.** You don't want anyone to not have a pair of running shoes if you want to hike! Better yet, you don't want someone packing cutoff shorts and a t-shirt for dinner if you made reservations at a fine dining restaurant!

- **Incorporate games and activities into your itinerary.** Everyone likes to be active and involved with each other and the bride. Giving the girls lots to do will keep the weekend from getting cliquish and drama-ridden. Cliques are less likely to form if the girls get to regularly interact as a group.

The Budget Bride

Ways to save money on your bachelorette party:

- Choose a location within driving distance.

- For large parties, it can be cheaper per person to hire a local chef to come to the house to prepare dinner instead of going out to a fine dining restaurant.

- Avoid activities that cost money to participate. Miami pool parties are fun but come with an entry fee. You can have just as much fun relaxing on the beach, free of charge!

- Stop at a grocery store and liquor store beforehand to stock the house. Having some breakfast foods and drinks at the house is always a good idea. Plus, drinks at home are always cheaper than drinks out!

For more photos, go to
www.thecovidbridebysara.com/post/bachparty

THE NEW WEDDING PLANNER

Around the time of my bachelorette party, communication with my wedding planner Madison stopped abruptly. Before Christmas break, Madison gave me tasks to do and told me we would connect after the new year to discuss the venue's restrictions. Hannah, the events coordinator at Braxton Country Club, had told us that the club was only allowing events for fifty or fewer guests.

I wanted to check back in to see if that was still the case because it would dramatically change the event that we'd invited over three hundred guests to. January fifth had rolled around, and I hadn't heard a peep from Madison or anyone from our venue.

I sent another email to Hannah and Madison to schedule a meeting at the club.

Someone at the country club read my email and called me immediately. "Hi, Sara, this is Kelly at Braxton County Club. Is this an okay time to chat?" her unfamiliar voice sounded shaky.

"Sure." I stepped away from the noisy TV in the living room at my parents' house.

"Hannah passed away a few weeks ago due to a rare genetic disease. It had nothing to do with COVID," Kelly muttered. "We apologize for the lack of correspondence on our end. We're still trying to get everything sorted out around here."

Overcome with deep sadness, I couldn't speak for a long moment. "I am so sorry to hear that. I...I can't believe it."

"I assure you that I will be able to take on your event from here on out. You have nothing to worry about," Kelly tried to reassure me.

"Oh, yeah...I'm not worried about that. How is her husband?" Hannah met her husband at BCC when she was the new event coordinator, and he was the head chef. I had met him during our food tasting.

"He is taking some time off right now. Thank you for asking," Kelly mumbled.

"Okay, well, I was calling to check up on the COVID policy to see if anything has changed. You have your hands full right now. Would you mind giving us an update when you can?" I asked.

"Our policy hasn't changed. The club will only allow up to fifty guests for any event," Kelly cautioned.

"Right. Well, I'm so sorry to hear about Hannah. I'll check back in shortly." I hung up the phone.

I was devastated, even though I had only known Hannah for a few months. I spent time with her during our initial food tasting, tours of the club, and other meetings. We had been in constant contact since July. I had just seen her a month ago. She was so young and beautiful!

Two stress-filled weeks later, I received an email from Madison's boss from Somethin' Blue Events.

To: Sara La Chapelle
From: Sage
Date: January 15, 2021, 12:18 p.m. EST
Subject: La Chapelle Wedding

Hi Sara & Peter,

I hope you are doing well and had a restful holiday. I am reaching out to let you know that I will be taking over as your Wedding Planner. Please email me, call/ text, or message via HoneyBook.

I have been reviewing your vendor files and communications with Madison and am excited to take over. I would love to schedule a time to chat next week once I'm back from my family vacation. Let me know what days/times work for you all.

Sage

I was so bewildered. What happened to Madison? Was she physically okay? If she had quit her job, why? I Googled Somethin' Blue Events to see if I could figure out what was going on.

The website returned a 404pagenotfound error. Their website was gone. That seemed shady, so I hopped onto Instagram and typed in their handle. Nothing came up. Their Facebook page was gone as well. Now I really had a lot of questions! Somethin' Blue Events had been utterly scraped from the digital world, which could **not** be a good sign.

I texted Madison asking if she was doing okay, but she never responded. The wedding planner I talked to nearly every day for the last nine months and considered a friend ghosted me.

Madison never told us goodbye, and we don't know what happened to make her abandon her clients. I would have been understanding if she had told us what was going on in her life. I couldn't shake the ominous omen cast by the tragic sudden death of my venue coordinator and my runaway wedding planner.

When I finally got Madison's business partner, Sage, on the phone a week later, she seemed stressed and on the verge of crying. I tried to ask about Madison to see if she was okay. Sage would not disclose any information about how Madison was or what happened between the two of them.

The next order of duty was to ask if Sage could collect my wedding RSVPs that were already printed to be sent to Madison's address in Athens, Georgia, two hours away from my Peachtree City apartment. Sage assured me that was not a problem, and she could collect them.

Once the small housekeeping tasks were out of the way, I asked Sage if she had the bandwidth to take on the workload of another wedding that was not originally on her schedule. "Braxton Country Club is only allowing fifty guests for weddings, and we will need to find another venue if they don't change their policy by the end of January. If I can't find another venue nearby that can accommodate my guest list, I'll need to reschedule the entire weekend of events." It was essential to ensure she had a grasp of the entire messy situation.

"I will honor the contract and follow through with our commitment to you," Sage insisted, resignation clear in her voice.

"Are you apprehensive about attending an event with at least two hundred guests since COVID is still an issue?" I asked.

"I'm not concerned with the virus, and I will fulfill my duties as your wedding planner," Sage promised.

I gave her an opening to quit multiple times, and she didn't take the bait. I was apprehensive that her heart was no longer in wedding planning. She had erased Somethin' Blue Events from the internet and wouldn't be accountable for doing a lousy job on my wedding now that she was dissolving her company.

If we had to change venues this late in the game, Sage would be responsible for essentially planning an entirely new wedding. She wouldn't be able to operate based on the existing notes in my file. To make matters worse, Kelly at BCC was also trying to get up to speed on my event after the passing of Hannah.

Since coming up with a Plan B was such a cumbersome undertaking, I asked Sage, "Would I be able to hire a wedding consultant to assist in the research of available venues for our alternate arrangements? That way, you can get up to speed on Plan A, and I can explore other options just in case."

"That would be a great idea!" Sage readily agreed.

After our phone call, I got on my computer and reached out to a wedding planner I had never spoken with before. I'd followed her Instagram account, Georgia Weddings, for months. I DMed the account and got a quick response from Margot, the lead planner, and set up a time to chat on the phone.

By the grace of God, Margot was available on May eighth and willing to step in where she could. The fact that she was available on my date was enough for me to beg for a contract. I described how I was looking to hire someone to discuss the overall logistics of a Plan B wedding and how she would need to work alongside my other planner, Sage.

A week later, in February, I set up a meeting with Sage from Somethin' Blue Events to introduce her to Margot. Everything sounded fine during our conference call, and I thought I had resolved the burden of Sage having to replan my entire wedding until I received her final email.

Sara and Peter,

After our conversation this morning, I feel that it is in everyone's best interest to allow your new consultant to take over your upcoming wedding. In addition to the complications of changing the venue and onboarding another consultant to work with Plan A, I have been struggling with mounting concerns for my safety and the safety of others with such a large guest count/event during COVID19.

I am happy to waive the final payment, should you agree that no further obligations remain under the Wedding Services Agreement.

Sage

Sage had quit. I had now lost **three** wedding planners. As a result, I would have to take on the tasks she'd agreed to do. Sage heartlessly advised us to download our budget Excel document, guest list, and vendor contracts because my account would be terminated within the next forty-eight hours.

Just when I thought I had wedding planning under control, I had to take on the task of organizing and coordinating my existing contracts. Upon obtaining those documents, it became clear how disorganized the budget and contracts actually were. It took me over nine hours to rework the budget and accurately input all of the money we had already spent toward the wedding. Over the next few weeks, I would be setting up appointments to tour new venues and rebuilding an event that would be taking place in three short months.

As far as the RSVP cards, Sage did not respond to my text messages asking if I could get them from her. It was too late to change the return address because the stationery company mailed them out the day before Sage quit.

At the end of the day, I never blamed Sage or Madison for going their separate ways. There was no manual on how to proceed with life during a pandemic, and navigating a business was even more uncertain. Wedding planning during COVID brought unforeseen hurdles. Planners were having to replan their clients' big days, and they were not getting compensated for that time.

Wedding Planner Advice

- **Work alongside your wedding planner:** This day is too momentous to rely on a stranger to do it all for you. Ask for help when you need it, but be involved in the process. It wasn't until my wedding planner shut down her business that I actually reviewed the budget in detail and read my vendor contracts.

- **Don't outsource tasks you can do on your own:** I learned that I could have planned most of my wedding by myself. I took on the responsibility for all the extra tasks I hired my original wedding planners to do. I created my own design and wedding website, and I purchased and assembled all Seventy-five welcome gifts and one hundred and fifty party favors. When it came to my wedding, taking on the tasks of coordinating the little things gave me peace of mind.

- **Review the scope of work you agreed upon.** Continually review the agreement you made with your wedding planner to make sure they are completing the tasks agreed upon. On the other hand, don't ask your planner to take on tasks not originally outlined without updating your contract. There should be no passive responsibilities but a clear outline of who does what to ensure nothing falls through the cracks.

The Budget Bride

Hire a wedding planner that gets paid a flat fee instead of a percentage of your budget. If you have a $100,000 budget or a $50,000 budget, the time the planner commits to your event should be the same. If your budget leaves little wiggle room for a full-time wedding planner, you can hire planners to complete specific tasks you need assistance with by pricing out à la carte options. Examples of tasks you may need help with could include ceremony or reception design, vendor coordination, or rehearsal dinner planning.

THE BRIDAL SHOWER

I got off on the wrong foot with Peter's family a long time ago. I met Peter's parents, his brother, Sophia (his brother's girlfriend at the time), plus a few of his cousins, over Labor Day weekend three years ago in Rehoboth Beach, Delaware. It was actually before our first official date. We had only known each other for a week and a half when he invited me to his family's beach house for the weekend.

I rationalized that going to the beach with a virtual stranger was an acceptable risk because I needed to make friends in my new city. However, I'm not completely devoid of a sense of self-preservation, and I only agreed to go if I could bring my girlfriend, Kim. Kim had moved to DC after college to work for the mayor. She was my lifeline and home away from home. She agreed to the weekend trip, so we set off on our two-hour journey from my apartment to Delaware.

By the end of the weekend, I thought I had made new best friends and couldn't wait to hang out with Peter, his brother Daniel, and Sophia when we all returned to DC. But apparently, I was mistaken! On the ride home, Kim told me that Sophia was throwing shade at us the **entire** weekend. She overheard Sophia judging me while I napped outside on the dock following an afternoon of day drinking. I came for a good time, not a long time. I was too busy cutting loose to notice any potential judgment; I figured I'd made a solid first impression.

Eight months later, I met the rest of Peter's family in Rehoboth Beach over Easter weekend. When I arrived at the beach house in my matching two-piece outfit, I confidently introduced myself to Peter's sister Emily and his aunt Elle, both of whom I had never met. Seconds after introducing myself to Emily and Elle, the room became awkwardly quiet. I immediately thought I had spinach in my teeth, or better yet, **loser** written across my forehead. The tension was so apparent it could be cut with a dainty butter knife. For the rest of the weekend, I felt like I was the elephant in the room.

Peter told me that Sophia voiced her genuine concerns for him taking an interest in me because of my outlook on casual dating, meaning I couldn't be taken seriously. Ever since that Easter weekend three years ago, I have felt like an outsider amongst his family.

Around Thanksgiving holiday after our engagement, Peter's family members gathered at his parents' beach house in Rehoboth Beach. My bridal shower became a topic of conversation amongst the women in his family. Despite Sophia's disinterest, the final consensus was that ten of Peter's female family members wanted to come to my shower to show their support.

I thought this was a very sweet gesture considering I still had no idea how they felt about me. I was stunned Peter's family wanted to travel from Los Angeles and Delaware for a dinky afternoon tea party. I hadn't planned for out-of-town guests, but I am a the-more-the-merrier kind of gal.

After hearing this news, I immediately went into party-planning mode. I began quizzing Peter on the number of guests, their addresses, if they had someplace to stay in Atlanta, and what dietary restrictions I needed to relay to the caterer. This was my chance to host his family and get to know them better. If they only got to know me, surely they would warm up to me and leave the past behind.

At the beginning of September, I began planning the bridal shower my mother offered to host. I ordered fifty custom bridal shower invitations from Cotton Lilies. My shower would take place on Sunday, February fourteenth, from two to five o'clock in the evening. There would be incredible food, darling decorations, and my friends would wear red or pink to match the theme. For the ladies with Valentine's Day dates, an event ending at five allowed plenty of time to make it to dinner with their beaux.

I had the slightest bit of relief when my pageant coach, Mrs. Olivia, reached out to my mom to see if she could co-host my shower. She had previously hosted the bridal shower for the former Miss Georgia and had boxes of decorations we could use for my party. I felt honored that Mrs. Olivia wanted to be a part of my event. Not only is she an incredible party planner, but her blessing meant a lot to me.

As the party date of February fourteenth approached, I became a stress ball trying to onboard my new wedding planner, Margot. Simultaneously, COVID infections were rising again, making planning even more problematic. Everyone in my family came down with COVID at one point or another, including my eighty-six-year-old grandparents. We are all fine now, if you're wondering.

Instead of relying on my mother and Mrs. Olivia to coordinate during a pandemic, I arranged the main details on my own. I created the guest list, designed the invitations, handwrote each address, stamped them, mailed them, followed up with the RSVPs, coordinated the caterer, hired the photographer, and purchased the spirits and remaining décor. The decorations were red, pink, white, and gold. I created a menu with Platinum Catering, inspired by traditional British high tea with finger foods like crustless cucumber sandwiches, pimento cheese on croissants, and chocolate-covered strawberries. I even crafted a Valentine's pink signature cocktail.

Everything was coming together. I was excited for my girlfriends to meet Peter's family before the wedding.

As the shower date approached, I started to receive RSVPs with regrets due to concerns over COVID. Out-of-town guests were waiting for a vaccine before engaging in social gatherings. Peter's mom informed me that she would still be there, and she was sorry to hear her family couldn't make it.

Daniel, Peter's best man, told him he would visit Valentine's weekend **no matter what.** He wanted to come to Atlanta to visit Peter, meet his new friends, and discover where we had been living since the beginning of COVID. Peter was so thrilled for his brother to visit that he rented a party room at a local brewery near our apartment to host a more official gathering while the bridal shower was taking place.

A few days before the bridal shower, Sophia texted Daniel, Peter, and me.

Hi Sara and Peter. Hope you are doing well. Just wanted to reach out to check in about your shower, Sara. Since I have to go into the office every day, I'm very hesitant about attending any sort of event right now but we absolutely want to find a way to show our support for you both.

Would you be okay with celebrating with us in Atlanta the night or day before instead? We'd still fly out to see you guys, I just wouldn't attend the shower. I know it's a big day for you, Sara so I absolutely don't want to step on your toes with this request! If doing a smaller thing that weekend doesn't work, we're happy to fly out another weekend instead. Just let us know.

This was a **huge** ask! My bridal shower was planned for Sunday, and I expected to be setting up for the event all day Saturday. I had my hands full the week beforehand. On top of preparing for the bridal shower, onboarding my **fourth** wedding planner, and identifying new potential venues, I still had a full-time job. But Peter hadn't seen his brother in months, and I wasn't going to let this possibility slip away. I had to do everything in my power to make sure Daniel would visit Georgia to visit Peter.

Hey Sophia!! Sure, come on down!!! I can't guarantee that your flights to or from ATL will be safe. I know

Delta is the only airline seating half capacity, so I'd check their tickets first.

Also, I can't guarantee that going out to dinner on Friday or Saturday would be the level of COVID-cautious you are looking for. Sophia, let me know how we can accommodate you. I know Peter is looking forward to hanging with Daniel while the girls are at the shower.

I scrambled to set up a weekend for Daniel and Sophia that was COVID-safe. I took off from work on Thursday and Friday to decorate my parents' house for the shower, knowing I'd be immersed in entertaining Peter's family on Friday and Saturday. I cleaned our apartment and went shopping for hors d'oeuvres and cocktails to host everyone. I called around until I found a private room I could rent for my immediate family and Peter's family to dine together on Saturday before Daniel and Sophia headed out of town.

After all of my effort to include Peter's family, it ended up being just his mom who came to the shower that weekend. I never expected his family to travel for a bridal shower during a pandemic, but I was disappointed that COVID stood in the way of hosting Peter's family in a more intimate gathering.

My bridal shower ended up being a blast, and it was well worth the effort. My family and friends outdid themselves and purchased everything on my registry! I had to register for more wedding gifts after that weekend's generosity. Since Peter's family couldn't attend the party, they shipped gifts to my house beforehand and emailed me a virtual signed card. They went out of their way to express their support from afar.

Toward the tail end of the bridal shower, Peter and his friends came from the brewery to continue the party at my parents' house. The men and women mingled until 10:00 p.m., reveling with wine on a school night!

© Lane Creatore

Bridal Shower Advice

- **Take superficial support with a grain of salt.** The people in your life who truly care about you will always be there for the things that are important to you, not just what **they** deem is important. Keep that in mind and show up for the people you care about to the events that matter to them, even if they don't matter much to you. I felt so loved and supported that afternoon, surrounded by my family and friends and even Peter's family from a distance. The people who attended the shower are the same people who have continued to encourage Peter and me since day one. They are the people who know us as a couple and care if our marriage succeeds.

- **Publicly announce a thank you to those who hosted the event.** In the middle of the event, somewhere after food has been served and before games or gift opening begins, thank your hosts in front of everyone. You don't need to give a long speech, just a few words of appreciation for hosting the event.

The Budget Bride

Consider borrowing decorations or using a holiday theme to cut back on décor. My Valentine's Day-themed bridal shower made it possible to repurpose decorations we already owned, as well as borrow from others. You could play off Halloween, Easter, the Fourth of July, or other holidays with their own set of decorations.

For more photos, go to
www.thecovidbridebysara.com/post/shower

THE PLAN B

By February, I knew I needed to find another venue. Braxton Country Club, the venue of my dreams, was adamant about restricting the number of wedding guests to fifty. I wanted to hold on to the possibility that the new COVID vaccine would hit the market and restrictions would be lifted, but BCC assured me they did not see themselves changing their policy in the foreseeable future.

There was no way I could cut my guest list of three hundred and twenty-five guests down to fifty, and I couldn't wait any longer for an increasingly unlikely change in my favor. Wanting to move forward with my life, I refused to postpone the wedding. The future of COVID was still unknown and unpredictable, and I feared the world could be in an even worse place in another year.

Initially, our first thought was to host the wedding in my parents' backyard. Their Greek Revival mini-mansion sits on a couple acres of land in the suburbs. We could eliminate the rules and restrictions of a public venue if we hosted the wedding at our private residence.

We could build a temporary deck, throw up a clear tent, and string twinkle lights. The biggest hurdle would be wrangling together last-minute vendors to rent tables, chairs, glassware, plates, cutlery, and everything else the country club would have provided. In addition to the tablescape, we would need to rent a dance floor, stage, fancy mobile restrooms, and a generator to power the event.

My dad was willing to hear out the idea of shifting the nuptials to his backyard, but with enough time and close consideration, he came to despise the idea. "Sara, I don't want to be held liable for the event. If anyone gets COVID, they can sue us!" My dad shook his head.

"We can administer rapid COVID tests at the door, or we can make our vendors sign a waiver." I did my best to sell the idea.

My dad shot down the idea, so I went back to the drawing board. My new wedding planner, Margot, my mom, and I came up with a shortlist of viable options for a Plan B. The wedding was only four months away.

Since the city of Atlanta had stricter COVID protocols than the suburbs, I explored the idea of hosting the wedding in the historic town of Senoia. For those of you who are unfamiliar with this area, it is located thirty minutes from the city of Atlanta. There is a great downtown area, called Main Street, lined with pre–Civil War buildings, boutiques, and highly coveted restaurants. Main Street looks like something out of a Hallmark movie.

Shifting the wedding to Senoia was logistically burdensome, faced with the obstacle of rescheduling a jam-packed, three-day wedding weekend extravaganza. If we found a venue in Senoia, we would need to change our rehearsal dinner location, find another church, reserve the bed and breakfast down the street, and shift all of our vendor contracts to a new location. Switching the entire wedding weekend to take place in the suburbs wasn't the best option either because we'd lose the down payments we made for the church and rehearsal dinner in Midtown.

Peter's and my desire to get married on May eighth outweighed the financial risk involved in switching venues. We were willing to do anything—including revising the entire weekend—if it meant we could still get married on our date.

I pulled the trigger and sent an email to BCC, canceling our reservation.

To: Kelly, Braxton Country Club
From: Sara La Chapelle
Date: February 9, 2021, at 11:30 a.m. EST
Subject: Unfortunate Termination of BCC Contract

Dear Kelly,

After twelve months of meticulous planning, we are having to cancel our wedding at Braxton Country Club due to COVID19 restrictions.

First and foremost, I would like to thank you and our sponsor for your efforts in securing our date, especially during a pandemic.

I had always dreamed of hosting a wedding reception at BCC, but circumstances have changed, and we are doing our best to salvage the event.

Thank you for your time,
Sara La Chapelle

The weekend after canceling our BCC reservation, Peter and I began touring other venues. I made appointments to tour The Rockstone Mill and Wylie Hall because both venues had our date available and had loose COVID restrictions.

Rockstone Mill is a rustic venue located on the Chattahoochee River that runs through Georgia. The venue is surrounded by old Senoia bars and restaurants that have character. Rolling up for our tour, I was immediately unimpressed by the maroon wooden building. The entire establishment reminded me of where I had my eighth-grade dance. Peter and I walked into the front door and were greeted by the owner. "My husband and I own this venue. He is the lead chef, and I take care of the business aspects!" she explained.

Within seconds of looking around our top contending venue, my dream of a Vogue-style wedding flew out the window. I couldn't get past the moldy, campy smell associated with old wood near water. The ceilings were nine feet tall at most and lined with outdated wrought iron light fixtures and rows of Edison light bulbs. The windows were treated with heavy black drapes, and the hallway to the bathroom was painted a bleak forest green. I wouldn't have used their dark wooden folding chairs for a backyard BBQ. Let's just say they were no gold Chiavari.

The venue could not have been more dissimilar from the posh, French-style chateau we'd initially booked. Peter commented on the juxtaposition of BCC to The Rockstone Mill.

Since we had never toured secondary options for the wedding, he was oblivious to what other venues looked like.

The Rockstone Mill was not for us. But like true Southerners, we respectfully sat through the entire pitch and collected the menu and pricing. Before heading to our next tour, we thanked our kind event coordinator and headed toward the door as quickly as we could.

Next, we toured Wylie Hall, located on Main Street, less than a mile from our apartment. It was built in the 1840s and had a lot of similarities to my parents' house. Both were Greek revival homes with white columns, a front porch, and a lot of great land for entertaining. When Peter and I ascended the steps toward the front door, a blonde lady with a sweet Georgia accent invited us into the grand foyer, the main entryway with black-and-white marble floors, placed in between two sitting rooms. This architectural style of a library and parlor off the grand foyer is common in older Southern homes.

I immediately liked the spirit of Wylie Hall a thousand times better than Rockstone Mill—there was no campy smell in the old house, despite its historic founding. The furniture was in great condition and had recently been updated. The interior décor caught me off guard; the pieces were Southern vintage but high quality and well selected.

Wylie Hall could have been a possible option for us, but Peter and I decided against it because we would need to rent a tent in the front of the house for additional seating. The ballroom was rather small and could hardly fit our extravagant head table of forty people, plus the stage for our twelve-piece band. Where would our guests dance? Where would we do our first dance? Where would everyone eat dinner? I noted the inconveniences that went along with this venue.

If nothing else were available, we could go with Wylie Hall. "There is a lot of potential for setting up multiple seating areas and a tent," I told Peter. "We can make it beautiful, but I'm concerned that we are going to lose the energy with everyone spread out. It would be difficult, if not impossible, for everyone to enjoy the little things happening like the cake cutting, speeches, or first dances."

Feeling discouraged, Peter and I headed back to our apartment to review our options. Did we host our wedding in the rustic, camp-like venue or in a tent and spread through multiple rooms in a historic estate?

I called my mom in a panic. "Wylie Hall could be lovely, but the layout of the venue doesn't handle our large guest list well."

"Don't worry. I'll come up with other options," she vowed.

I was beginning to fret because the wedding was only three months away at this point, and most venues were booked by now.

On Monday morning, my mother called me from Palm Beach with positive news. She had sent inquiries to ten hotels and venues in Atlanta and received a call back from two. "The Brantley Hotel in Midtown and the Egyptian Ballroom at the Apollo Theatre are both still available for May eighth. Why don't you go check them out?"

As a former thespian and musical theater nerd, I thought the Apollo Theatre would be quite fitting. When I was younger, I performed the Nutcracker for a season at the venue with a professional dance studio.

I was thirty minutes into my drive to Midtown from the suburbs when I got a call from the coordinator at the Apollo Theatre. "I am so sorry, but I thought May eighth was a Sunday. We are booked on Saturday, May eighth, but I have Sunday, May ninth, available!"

"Oh, we want to try to keep our date. Thank you anyway." I turned my car around to drive back to Peachtree City.

After spending an uneventful hour in the car, I settled on my couch to do more research. The second I snuggled up with my laptop and a blanket, I got a call from The Brantley Hotel.

"Hi, Sara, this is Pierre from The Brantley Hotel." His French accent caught me off guard. "I spoke with your mother earlier, and she told me you were interested in our venue for May eighth. When would you like to come in?"

"Hi, thank you for calling," I replied. "I was wondering when I'd hear from you. I'd like to come in as soon as possible!"

"We have an opening this afternoon. When could you be here?" Pierre asked.

I looked at the time. It was past 3:00 p.m., and I knew I would get caught in rush hour traffic on my way home, but I was desperate. "I can be there in an hour!" I slipped on my shoes, threw on my black puffer jacket, grabbed a granola bar, and headed back out the door.

The Brantley Hotel's ballroom was far from complete, but it was better than anything else we'd seen. The biggest selling point was that we could fit everyone in the ballroom at the same time. With a large dance floor at the center of the room, no one would miss a beat. In addition, the experienced staff could easily serve a sit-down dinner for over two hundred guests.

There was only one problem. It was drastically over my budget—by a lot. In addition to the increased price per person, I would have to spend a fortune transitioning the ballroom into a proper wedding venue. Unlike BCC, The Brantley Hotel did not include cake, drapery from the ceilings, a fancy dance floor, and statement bars that I could use for the cocktail hour. I would need to select and coordinate more vendors to achieve my vision.

By this point, our wedding invitations had already been sent out with the canceled venue and food selections that were not available at the hotel. Peter and I would have to schedule another food tasting to select our menu. No matter what venue we chose, we would still need to send another invitation with the updated information.

After the tour, I asked Pierre for a quote for guest counts of three hundred and twenty-five, two hundred and fifty, and one hundred and eighty-five. I wanted to see what I would financially be committing to depending on the number of guests that responded with a "gladly accept."

With all of this new information, I printed out the quotes and brought them to the head decision-maker, my father. I presented him with a packet of venue information and a pricing sheet in his office.

"Is The Brantley Hotel the best possible option?" My dad looked up from the paperwork and asked, his glasses at the tip of his nose.

"Yes, but before I sign the contract, I want to make sure they accept my changes I added: if the city of Atlanta or the state of Georgia imposes COVID restrictions on group gatherings, we would not be held liable and would be fully refunded our down payment." I handed him a copy of the contract with revisions.

"Will you be going over your wedding budget?" my dad asked haplessly.

"Yes. It's more expensive all-around." I circled the number on the bottom of the contract.

My dad nodded his head, and we didn't talk about it again.

I was desperate to secure the new venue, so I signed a contract committing myself, with a large down payment the very next day.

Letting go of BCC was galling, but I realized something when I finally let go. I was never supposed to get married there to begin with. Yes, I got approved by the board, but I wasn't a member, and I would have felt like an outsider. I already felt like I was walking on eggshells trying to schedule an event as a guest. On my wedding day, I would have felt like a poser, and no one wants to feel that way!

Switching to the hotel freed me from the oppressive rules of the country club. I wouldn't have to worry about getting in trouble if my guests tagged the venue on social media. I would be able to post as many photos of my wedding as I wanted. I could be published in a wedding magazine, or heck, I could even write a book about it!

Plan B Advice

- **Find a venue where you feel at home and connected.** You want to feel a sense of belonging and peace. Consider picking a place you and your spouse can visit again for an anniversary. There was no way I'd be able to pop in BCC in the future, but Peter and I intend to go back to The Brantley Hotel every so often to relive our wedding.

- **Efficiently find a new venue.** If you have to rebook your wedding, only tour venues that have room for your date and your guest list.

- **Be willing to compromise when selecting a new venue.** Whether it's COVID or your venue burned down, you are not going to find another venue that fits all of the criteria for your original venue. Focus on the aspects that align most with your event goals, and let go of the rest.

The Budget Bride

If you found a venue you love, but it's over your ideal price range, consider getting married on a cheaper day of the week. It's cheaper to host a wedding on a Sunday as opposed to a Saturday. If your venue choice dominates your budget, eliminate extras like party favors, make your own centerpieces, serve only beer and wine, or trim down your guest list.

THE FIRST FITTING

My dazzling diamond-white wedding gown sat in my parents' closet, where Peter couldn't catch a glimpse of it, for four months before it was time for alterations. The bridal shop had advised us to wait until two months before the wedding for the first round of alterations and the second round one month out. Far too often, brides gain or lose weight before their wedding, so it's best to hold off on alterations until closer to the wedding date.

On March first, I lugged my thirty-pound garment bag downstairs and placed it in the trunk of my mother's car. I was itching to see my gown again because I hadn't touched it since it arrived.

My mom and I returned to the bridal shop where I bought the gown, this time wearing well-fitting facemasks. They took our temperatures at the door and directed us toward the alterations department.

I bolted to the dressing room to slip on my gown, then waddled out and asked Sue, the alterations woman, to zip me up. She fastened the gown, and I enthusiastically moved toward the mirror.

I took one look at myself, and I couldn't wipe discomfort off my face. The gown I remembered ten months ago looked astoundingly different. When I bought the gown, I tried on a sample that was four sizes too big. My dress consultant used heavy-duty clips to create a suitable fit. The bigger sample provided **a lot** more coverage. I felt like I was wearing an entirely different gown; it was itchy around the bustline, heavy on my lower back, and way too low cut for a church ceremony! None of these issues had been present in the ivory sample I'd tried on.

I stepped closer to the mirror, pulling the gown along with me. I repeated in my head, *Lord, please let Sue fix this gown. Please let Sue fix this gown!*

It was going to need significant adjustments to fit properly, a feat that was possible but fraught with its own hazards. As a former pageant girl, I've worn dozens of gowns. Many were drastically improved by the alterations process, but many more had been destroyed with irreversible mistakes. Altering a custom gown that took six months to make cannot be taken lightly!

I warned Sue, "Let's be cautious with the first round of alterations. We can always take it in more later on. It's a lot harder to let it out."

Sue began pinching the gown at the bodice, the waist, and the hemline.

"Mom! Hello?" I tried to get my mom's attention. She was on the phone with someone in our family, but I wasn't sure who. "Mom, what do you think about this length? Is it too short? I want my gown to cover the tops of my shoes, but I don't want to be tripping on it either." I spoke louder, in an effort to get her to engage with me.

My mother dismissed my question and waved me off with her palm.

"I think that length looks right," I approved the hemline.

"What next?" Sue asked, letting me direct the adjustments.

Tugging at the strapless top, I complained, "The bodice is driving me crazy! Is there any way you can pin the gown to sit higher on my chest? I feel like I could flash someone if I raise my arms." I tested my theory, lifting my arms above my head, and I promptly flashed the boutique. "Oops! I was right," I snickered. It would be a lot less funny on my wedding day.

Sue and I continued to attack the remaining kinks of the dress. It needed to be hemmed, pinched at the waist, and clipped at the bust, bustled, and secured. After resolving the main issues, it took Sue twenty minutes to pin together my fifteen-foot-long train into a bustle. Watching Sue piece it together was like watching a surgeon working on a highly delicate patient.

Last, she placed ten pins to mark where she would sew small metal clips at my waistline to secure my tulle overskirt. I loved the option to remove my tulle overskirt, giving my gown two looks. Without the overskirt, my gown was a form-fitting, strapless column, but with the overskirt, it was dramatic, feminine, and more ballgown-ish.

My mom was still on the phone, speaking well over the appropriate indoor voice. "That's not a problem; we can seat you at a different table!" I still had no idea who she was talking to or what the issue was. I tried to get my mom off the phone by signaling "cut" at the top of my neck, but she was in her own world.

My mom finally hung up the phone. "That was your cousin Mario. He doesn't want to sit next to his brother Carlo because they haven't gotten along in years," she announced.

"Are you kidding me? That's what took you thirty minutes to discuss?" I was furious my family was requesting preferential treatment when I was dealing with a wedding during COVID. I guess family drama doesn't stop for a virus.

"Don't move!" Sue yelped. "You're bleeding on your gown. Don't move! Let me get a solution to clean it right away before it stains."

My body went cold. I looked down and saw a quarter-size drop of blood at the top of my gown. Apparently, I'd pricked my finger on a pin holding the gown in place.

Luckily, Sue was able to remove the stain before it could set. We paid a deposit for alterations and booked our final appointment four weeks out.

On our way out the door, I confessed to my mom, "There's no way I am going to be able to dance in that gown. When I ordered it, I didn't know Peter and I would have such an intricate first dance with spins, lifts, and dips." I hadn't taken my wedding dress into consideration while choreographing our dance.

"Why did you have to order an ungainly gown in the first place?" my mom interrogated me.

"I don't know! It felt really different when I tried on the sample!" I whined. "Please, can we find another gown I can wear just for my first dance?"

"Fine, but we aren't spending more than a couple hundred dollars on it." She folded like a cheap lawn chair. A huge sigh of relief washed over my tense body as my mother agreed to help me find another gown I could wear for our first dance.

Wedding Gown Alteration Advice

- **Know that sample gowns may fit differently.** When trying on sample gowns, note that larger sizes will have a more modest fit when clipped to your body. When taking measurements, express any concerns you have regarding coverage. If you like the modest fit of the sample gown, have them add fabric to fit the way you like.

- **Bring your wedding shoes with you to alterations.** For a proper hem, you need to have the shoes you'll be wearing with the dress.

- **Try your wedding shoes with your gown prior to alterations.** I ordered shoes that had jewel embellishments, and I had to return them because they kept snagging the hem of my gown.

- **Bring the undergarments you will wear with you to alterations.** Find a bra and panty combo that works! I wore nipple pasties and Spanx. You don't want to wait till the last minute for this, or you'll end up emergency shopping.

- **Be consistent with your diet and workout scheme.** Your body can change a lot from the first round of alterations to your final round in only four weeks. To avoid alteration issues, do your best to maintain your current weight and shape.

The Budget Bride

You do not need to alter your gown at the boutique where you purchased it! Many times, in-house alterations are more costly than going to another seamstress!

THE FIRST DANCE DRESS

I'd made the mistake of buying a restrictive gown that was breathtaking but not something I would be able to perform our choreographed dance in. I managed to sweet-talk my mom into allowing me to buy a second gown specifically for the dance.

"I'm not going to give you more than a couple hundred bucks for a second gown!" my mom proclaimed. "You are only going to wear it to perform your first dance. There's no point in spending a fortune on something you're only going to wear for a few minutes."

"I'd be happy with a fifteen-dollar gown, as long as I can dance in it!" I insisted. "That's all I care about."

After alterations, my mom and I looked in the basement of the bridal boutique at their Seventy-five-percent-off sample gowns. Sample gowns are usually a size 8/10 to fit most women and are massively discounted because they have been tried on hundreds of times. Not to mention, they are usually a season or two old.

In the drab boutique basement, I flipped through sample gowns to see if anything caught my eye. I was unimpressed by the selection and asked the gown consultant for help. "Do you have anything simple, light, and easy to move in?" Since this was a peculiar request, the sales consultant found only two gowns that fit my criteria.

The first gown was made of soft Spanish tulle. It was alluring but in poor condition.

"That does nothing for your body," my mom critiqued. "What else do they have?"

I headed back into the dressing room to try on the other option. The gown reminded me of an early 2000s satin halter top with a fit-and-flare silhouette. I didn't even need to come out of the dressing room to know it wasn't what I needed. Discouraged, I redressed and headed back home to Peachtree City.

We passed a bridal boutique on our way home, and I asked my mom if she'd pull in to check their samples.

"You better call first. You can't just walk-in anywhere these days," my mom cautioned.

It was fate! There was one appointment available in thirty minutes. I booked the appointment and gave them my credit card information to secure my spot. We arrived a swift fifteen minutes later and waited in the car until our appointment.

I went through the same motions of describing what I was looking for in a second gown. "It needs to be simple, comfortable, and cheap. We also need the gown to be ready in seven weeks."

Without further ado, the sales consultant, Lauren, began pulling aside gowns and asking for my approval. Before I could try on any of the gowns, she required confirmation from the designers that they could be available in seven weeks. Out of ten, only two of the gowns could be delivered on time.

I tried on the first gown and fell in love with it. It was subtle and felt good to move in. The bodice was an ivory lace with nude mesh underneath, and the skirt had a plunging leg slit. It was flattering and showed off my thin figure without being overly revealing.

The second gown was similar to the first one, but didn't have a leg slit, and the waist had a white belt that separated the straight skirt from the top. The belt made me look short-waisted rather than long and willowy.

"What's the price of the first gown?" I asked.

"With rush shipping, it's one thousand six hundred dollars. If you want this gown on time, I need to order it by tomorrow at the latest." Lauren hinted at the fact we were running out of time to find anything decent.

"Could you give my mother and me a moment to discuss the gown in private?" I softly requested.

The gown was way more than a couple hundred dollars, and I started to feel guilty.

My mom accepted the fact we would be spending more than she bargained for. "If you really love it, you can order it."

I immediately refused. "No! It's way too much! Why don't we look at another boutique tomorrow before deciding? We can hold off another day." We thanked Lauren for her time and promised we would make up our minds by tomorrow afternoon.

The very next morning at 10:00 a.m., I enlisted the help of my grandmother and mother to look for a dance dress at another bridal boutique six minutes away from my parents' house. I had never heard of The Veil before, but my wedding planner highly suggested it.

Everything at The Veil was seven hundred and fifty dollars. They carry sample gowns in all sizes but only in excellent condition.

Catherine, our gown consultant, took my measurements and informed me that I would fit into the gowns with a pink and blue sticker on the hanger. She then handed us plastic gloves to wear to preserve the gowns as we combed through the racks.

"I'm looking for a gown that is light, airy, and easy to move in," I explained, trying to get Catherine up to speed.

"You have one hour for your appointment," Catherine announced as she clicked start on her stopwatch. "People will stay here for hours and try on every gown in the shop if we don't stick to our hour appointments." She laughed anxiously.

We found twenty dresses to try on that fit my specific criteria.

I tried on all twenty gowns but kept coming back to a sparkly one with a plunging leg slit. As much as I loved this gown, I couldn't pull the trigger on spending $750 on the spot. I left the store empty-handed, exhausted, and famished. Over lunch, my mother and grandmother advised ordering a gown online because I could return it if I changed my mind.

Over the next three days, I looked at every white gown for sale on the Nordstrom, Bloomingdales, Neiman Marcus, Saks Fifth Avenue, and Bergdorf Goodman websites. Many of the sites listed a Mac Duggal gown fitting for my first dance, but it was sold-out across the board. I searched the web for the gown's style number and tracked down one available in my size. I went ahead and ordered it, not realizing it was nonrefundable.

Two weeks later, the gown arrived much later than expected. The color looked **nothing** like it did online. It was gold and not ivory, but still glamorous. I was happy with my choice and knew it would work for our dance. I only intended to wear my internet-purchased wedding gown for a few minutes. I'd slightly look like a guest at my own wedding, but that was A-okay with me. It was flattering, suitable for dancing, under my budget, and in my hands. I could cross this dress debacle off my list of things to do and move on with this task.

First Dance Dress Advice

- **Don't order a nonrefundable gown off the internet!**

The Budget Bride

To avoid needing a second gown or an outfit change, purchase a dress that you feel comfortable in! Make sure you can sit, stand, and move in the way you need to at your wedding and reception.

THE NEW VENUE

We officially switched the reception to The Brantley Hotel three months before our wedding date. This may seem like adequate time to plan a reception, but I worked up until six days before the wedding making final adjustments.

The Brantley Hotel was the only venue available without stringent COVID regulations that could accommodate our large guest list and was close enough to the rehearsal dinner venue and church.

Compared to the ballroom at Braxton Country Club, the hotel ballroom seemed like an ugly stepsister. In the broad daylight, the ballroom was **anything but special**. The ceilings were tall, but nothing monumental. The main chandelier was anchored on the left side of the ballroom, making the space asymmetrical and cramming the event to the left. A brassy brown fabric covered the walls, clashing with the blue, white, and grey-speckled carpets that reminded me of something you'd see in a movie theater back in the nineties. On the longer end of the ballroom, four small windows overlooked a parking lot.

A week and a half after signing the contract, I met Margot and Rebecca, my wedding planner and florist, to tour the venue and share my ideas for the design. "The first thing I want to do is alleviate some of this wall space. I was thinking we could hang drapes from the ceiling and along the back wall," I proposed. "What do you think?"

"I will need to check with The Brantley and see if they know a vendor that can do that for us," Margot remarked. Later, we found out there was a fee of one hundred dollars per hook to hang drapes from the ceiling.

"Next, I was thinking we should have uplights around the perimeter of the ballroom to create depth and ambiance," I suggested.

"We can do that! I think we use a warm white light," Rebecca affirmed, jotting down notes.

"Next, I was thinking about putting the green ivy boxwood wall here in front of the head table." I waved my hands at a space in the back of the room while I spoke.

"I love that idea. I could add an arrangement of florals on it," Rebecca offered.

I stood in the center of the ballroom and assessed the space. "I rented a black and white dance floor. I got the inspiration after binge-watching Bridgerton on Netflix." I worried the black and white dance floor would clash with my blush and gold theme, but I couldn't afford the all-white dance floor with our monogram in the center that I preferred.

Margot and Rebecca took detailed notes as we discussed every aspect of the room, from a seating vignette, linens, white bars, neon Trelenberg sign, and photo booth. My goal was to

cover up as much of the ballroom as possible with sumptu-
ous drapes, a big dance floor, and tall centerpieces to draw
people's attention upward. I was concerned about how the
ballroom would look, but Margot and Rebecca reassured me
that everything would be **fine**.

My parents missed that initial design meeting with Margot
and Rebecca. They weren't able to tour the venue until March
eleventh for the food tasting. Since they accompanied me to the
tasting at BCC, we could use our experience to our advantage.

Before the tasting, I guided my parents through the space.
During the tour, I held back from sharing my vision and the
plans already set in motion. I wanted them to see the space
before I tried to share what I had in mind to fix it. In the
South, we call that "putting lipstick on a pig." My mother
was unusually quiet. Even my dad didn't have anything to say
about the ballroom, and he is usually the voice of optimism.
They were extra careful not to say anything that would unravel
my façade of stability.

I did my best to paint a picture of my vision, but it was too
abstract to describe. To be fair, I didn't have a clue how the
ballroom would turn out on the day of the wedding. It was
going to be a surprise for everyone!

After our tour, I headed to the dining room with my parents.
Our food tasting at BCC seemed gourmet and impressive at
the time, but after experiencing the menu at The Brantley
Hotel, I was convinced that our new venue had better food
and wine across the board. In fact, the wine and signature
cocktail options were so tasty, my mom and I polished off four
(maybe five) drinks before 5:00 p.m.

I thoroughly enjoyed the tasting, and I wasn't thinking about the fact I had scheduled premarital counseling that evening with Grace Christian Church. On our way home from The Brantley, I was so full and over-served that I laid horizontally in the backseat of my mother's SUV as our designated driver, my dad, drove us home.

Everything seemed to be on the right track until **two weeks** before the reception.

New Venue Advice

- **Add floor lighting for ambiance.** Most of the time, your venue or florist already will have lights you can use. Create depth and interest in the room by dimming the overhead lights and balancing the room with floor lights.

- **Enhance the room with candles.** Candles add more than atmosphere. They are romantic, tranquil, and make a major impact on your overall design. Candles are versatile and can be added anywhere—on a church altar, floating in a pool, in a fireplace, down the aisle, or evening hanging. If you are going to place them on the floor, use an LED battery-powered candle to avoid mishaps. Don't be afraid to mix tall candelabras, cylinder pillars, small votives, and even tea lights to enhance tables.

- **Add drapery to the walls and ceilings.** Ballrooms aren't known for their particularly appealing wallcoverings. To conceal unwanted walls or section-off cavernous space, drape the room with gauze-like fabric. This trick creates an upscale look and intimate mise-en-scène.

The Budget Bride

There are lots of ways to enhance your reception space on a budget! My favorite way to spruce up an event is through colorful table linens. The charge is about the same to rent pink table linens as for sequined or patterned ones! Dress up your event by choosing bold table linen to elevate the overall look. You can even mix and match up to three complementary fabrics by selecting a pattern, a solid, and an embellishment.

THE GRACE CHRISTIAN COUNSELING

While Peter and I prepared for our Catholic ceremony that would take place the week after our official wedding day, we simultaneously prepared for our ceremony at Grace Christian Church. We fell in love with this well-known gothic cathedral in the heart of Atlanta because of its breathtaking stained-glass windows, old-world European feel, and accessibility to our venue (both the original and new one).

Approximately two months before our wedding date, Dianne, the wedding coordinator at Grace Christian, assigned Reverend Willard to be our minister. He would work with us on our premarital counseling requirements, as well as officiate our ceremony. A little traumatized from our experience with the Catholic church, Peter and I were unsure about learning our new requirements.

With no time to spare, I immediately thanked Dianne for the contact and sent the reverend an email to schedule our first meeting. Reverend Willard promptly responded and explained the process to follow. Peter and I would need three hours of face-to-face counseling, in addition to a compatibility exam and some light reading.

I thought to myself, *What a piece of cake!*

To make things even easier on us, Reverend Willard offered Zoom appointments because of COVID. This was great for us because Peter's rigorous work schedule left little time for evening activities that didn't include eating or sleeping.

We scheduled our first Zoom counseling session the following Thursday at 7:30 p.m. Although common in the COVID19 era, it felt bizarre to meet our officiant for the first time remotely. Whenever I meet someone virtually for the first time, I can't help but wonder what I look like on their computer screen. Am I as charming as I am in real life?

By mistake, I scheduled our first meeting the same day as our food tasting at The Brantley Hotel. Peter had been excused from attending the tasting earlier that afternoon. It was essential for us to make a terrific first impression with our officiant. Unfortunately, I was in no condition to do so after polishing off five cocktails an hour earlier.

Reverend Willard kicked off the meeting. "Hi, Sara and Peter. Thanks for meeting with me tonight. I want to go ahead and let you know this experience is going to be informal. The purpose is for me to get to know you better before your ceremony. I like to get to know my couples well before marrying them! Why don't you and Peter begin with telling me about yourselves?"

Peter was the first to talk. He gave a detailed backstory on his life, sequentially talking through his time in New Jersey,

Houston, Hong Kong, Dallas, Los Angeles, and then DC, where we met.

When it was my time to share my story, I rambled on about unrelated events and my less-desirable attributes, like a scared child in confession. My childhood is a little fuzzy because I grew up in the same house most of my life. I was downright embarrassed and perceivably a little tipsy from the food tasting. By the end of the session, I had no idea what I told him about my life, but I was praying he wouldn't use anything embarrassing during our ceremony.

As the call ended, Reverend Willard gave us some homework to complete before our next meeting. "I am going to email you an article called 'Masters of Love' by Emily Esfahani Smith to read and discuss next week. In addition, click on the link in the email to take the forty-five-minute relationship exam that will encompass your strengths and weaknesses as a couple, relationship dynamics, personal stress profile, couple map, family map, and personality scales. We will go over your results together."

A week and a half later, we scheduled our next meeting with the reverend, and in that short timeframe, our ceremony plans came crashing down.

We received an email update from Dianne at Grace Christian Church:

To: Sara La Chapelle
From: Dianne Button
Date: Sunday, March 28, 2021, 1:50 p.m. EST
Subject: Re: La Chapelle Wedding COVID policy

The church leadership made a change to our COVID19 policy this week. Our **guest limit is set at the number 50** for right now. We will continue to monitor and amend the guidelines as conditions indicate.

Dianne

Finding another location for our ceremony was unavoidable, but I was terrified to ask the reverend if he would consider marrying us at a nonreligious establishment. Peter and I had already been denied by the Catholic church to co-host our ceremony, and I wasn't mentally prepared to be told again that God's children could not be married for some outdated reason. I was unsure how Reverend Willard felt about officiating events larger than fifty guests.

The morning before our second Zoom meeting with Reverend Willard, I began discussing potential ceremony options with The Brantley Hotel. The hotel confirmed that we could use their rooftop terrace for a ceremony space since we had already reserved it for cocktail hour. I was delighted to know that we had another option, but I wasn't ready to pull the trigger until I knew I had someone to officiate the ceremony. Shifting the church ceremony to the hotel would further break my budget, requiring rentals to transform their urban, concrete rooftop into a romantic ceremony venue.

Since we had not confirmed a new ceremony venue, I told Peter not to mention anything about it until the end of our final two-hour meeting with the reverend. I hoped that if Peter and I played our cards right, the reverend would have a hard time denying our request.

At the end of our final Zoom session with Reverend Willard, I politely asked, "Reverend, I hate to ask, but I got an email from Dianne telling us that the church is limiting the number of guests to fifty people. Well, that wouldn't even include Peter's family traveling **all the way** from California. I was wondering if you would be open to officiating our ceremony at The Brantley Hotel. I haven't made adjustments yet; I am waiting to see if the church changes their policy before replanning the ceremony."

"I will speak with the church and consider this request. I'm sorry you are having to deal with this," Reverend Willard apologized.

Peter and I patiently waited a week for his affirmative reply.

The Budget Bride

If you expect to get married by a nonreligious officiant, you most likely won't have to sign up for premarital counseling. Arranging premarital counseling on your own can be costly; marriage counselors charge anywhere from sixty to two hundred dollars an hour. If you want to prepare for marriage without the fees, I urge you to download one of my favorite relationship-strengthening apps called Gottman Card Decks. This app is free of charge and provides more than a thousand helpful questions, statements, and ideas for improving your relationship.

THE RSVPS

By the time our guests received our precious invitations, none of the information was correct, with the exception of our wedding date of May eighth. This is not to say I didn't dedicate adequate time proofreading the content. In the two weeks after our invitations were mailed, our venue had changed, the food options were different, and the RSVP cards were being mailed to my first wedding planner, who ghosted us. My wedding planner's business partner Sage agreed to forward our RSVPs but had become unresponsive.

I connected with Heather at Cotton Lilies to quickly draft a change-of-venue card to inform guests that our reception would now take place at The Brantley Hotel instead of Braxton Country Club. By the time Heather popped our change-of-venue cards in the mail, we had officially changed our ceremony from Grace Christian Church to The Brantley Hotel, making them only fifty percent relevant and a waste of $1,000.

Before Sage retracted her commitment to plan our wedding, she agreed to collect the RSVP cards from Madison. Our invitations were starting to be delivered, so I texted Sage with a heads up.

Sara: *Hi Sage, my invitations were mailed. Would you be able to grab the RSVPs from Madison and forward them to my home address?*

A week went by, and crickets. I figured she was busy with taking on the additional weddings that Madison dumped on her when she quit. Surely Sage would text me back as soon as RSVP cards started to roll in, but another week passed, and I still hadn't heard from her, so I sent another quick text.

Sara: *Hey Sage! Did you receive any of my RSVPs? Let me know if I can come get them.*

Days went by, and still no response from Sage. People began to receive our invitations and praised their beauty! Friends of mine told me they dropped their RSVP in the mail the same day they got the invite. It was time to collect my RSVPs, and I could no longer wait for Sage to text me back.

I called her number. Busy signal. I called again. Busy signal. *Beep, beep, beep.*

Sage had disconnected her phone. I sent her an email, but it bounced back. I had no way of contacting her, and it looked like I wouldn't be getting my RSVPs.

My mother was hysterical. "Get in the car, Sara! We are driving to Athens and knocking on the door your invitations are being mailed to!"

"Mom, it's a P.O. address. I don't have Sage's address," I declared.

"Then we'll call the Athens' police. Give me her number!" she shouted.

"I already told you, it's disconnected."

I reached out to all of the vendors Sage and Madison had connected me with and asked if they had any way of contacting my former wedding planners. I explained how my RSVP cards were being held hostage. It was an utter mess. People were sending in RSVP cards, and I had no way of receiving them.

My mom was determined to track down Sage and Madison. I stopped her from filing a report with the Athens police and then shut down her plans of hiring a private investigator. "Mom, I'll just call everyone on my invite list and ask them if they are coming to the wedding and what they want to eat."

This made my mom angrier. "Sara! Why would you send out an invite and then call for the responses! It is rude! Also, it is not the RSVP deadline for another three weeks."

The next idea I had was creating an RSVP option on our wedding website. Instead of going the traditional wedding website route, I designed my own custom site months prior. I thought it would look nicer but hadn't taken advanced functionality into consideration. I found a way to embed an event option on the site and pointed our landing page to an RSVP popup. I am not the most skilled web designer, but I was able to make a basic RSVP option.

I texted my guests the link to the wedding website with a short message. *Hello! Our RSVP cards are being mailed to an incorrect address. Please RSVP online. P.S. The seafood option has changed.*

For the most part, our guests were understanding with sending a second RSVP, but introducing a new RSVP option was time-consuming. Many calls required individual conversations with curious guests who wondered what happened to the RSVPs and our wedding planner and why scallops were no longer available.

RSVP Advice

- **Collect your own RSVPs.** I can't stress this enough! You will want to check your mailbox every day and see who said "Yes" to your wedding.

- **Include all the necessary components.** Sending a self-addressed, stamped paper RSVP makes it easier for guests to send in their responses.

- **Provide an option to RSVP online.** The younger generation will prefer an online RSVP, and the older generation will prefer to send theirs in by mail.

  - **Pro tip:** When creating your wedding website, use Zola, The Knot, or another service that provides wedding templates. It's not worth creating a custom site. Save your web design skills for your job, and don't waste them on this. It's a cinch to collect RSVPs from wedding websites, as they have built-in applications or modules to do this.

The Budget Bride

Instead of purchasing RSVP cards, envelopes, and postage, cut costs by requiring an online RSVP. Wedding websites like Zola and The Knot have options to embed an online RSVP that allows guests to respond by typing in their first and last name.

THE CATHOLIC CEREMONY

Months earlier, Peter and I **thought** we had completed our premarital counseling for our private Catholic ceremony to take place after our wedding.

One month prior to our planned Catholic ceremony, I got an email from Betty at St. Rita's Catholic Church.

To: Sara La Chapelle
From: Betty, St. Rita's
Subject: Wedding – May 11th
Date: Monday, April 12, 2021, 11:43 a.m. EST

Hi Peter and Sara,

Are you still planning on your May 11th ceremony? I don't have a copy of the certificate that shows completion of your wedding preparation. Please send it over ASAP.

God bless,
Betty

I immediately replied:

Hi Betty,

We have all of our paperwork: we completed the exam, attended a follow up meeting, and completed all 12 lessons in the workbook that was given to us at our first meeting. Do you want a copy of the workbook?

Best,
Sara

Betty replied:

Sara, I think you are confused. I still need quite a bit of paperwork for your wedding. I need:

1. Original baptism certificates for each of you.
2. Freedom to marry affidavits for each of you.
3. Wedding information sheet.
4. Workshop certificate from the Archdiocese.

God Bless,
Betty

On receipt of the email, I frantically called Peter at work to ask if he had any idea of what Betty was talking about.

"I'm not sure. I kept the paperwork on my desk in a folder labeled Catholic ceremony. Could you go grab it?" he asked.

I opened the folder, and there it was in bold letters. I read out loud:

> The couple will need to complete 20 hours of additional preparation either through the online curriculum available at catholicmarriageprep.com, or they can sign up for in-person workshops to complete their hours over two weekends. To sign up for a workshop, go to www. catholicmarriageprep.com/workshopnearyou

I lost my temper. "Peter, how could you miss this!? You were supposed to be in charge of this task! I've had my hands full with everything else!"

"Sara, I am so sorry," Peter apologized. "You know I've been distracted with my new job. I can look into it now and see what we can do."

We perused the Catholic Marriage Prep website together over the phone.

"It says the next workshop is May twenty-second and twenty-third. And the next workshop after that isn't until the middle of June! We are going to have to push our Catholic ceremony back a few months," I cried.

Peter found a loophole. "We can pay an extra $300 to complete the twenty-hour credit with a rushed online course.

Do you want me to sign up for that? A sponsor couple will review our assignments within twenty-four hours."

We paid $300 for the express course to avoid postponing our Catholic ceremony. I started it that afternoon. After four hours, I emailed my boss and announced that I needed to wrap up my current projects in order to focus on my wedding. The first of ten assignments took me eight hours to complete. My wedding was a month away, and nothing was under control.

The twenty-hour marriage course took me forty hours to complete. Since Peter couldn't dedicate his work hours to completing it, I completed it for the both of us. Once I finished all ten assignments, I dedicated two weekends teaching Peter the modules and reviewing our feedback from the sponsor couple.

Between Grace Christian Church and St. Rita's Catholic Church, Peter and I had spent:

- Two hours for an initial information meeting in the Catholic church

- Two hours for a follow-up appointment with the Catholic church

- Two hours collecting four affidavits from both of our parents

- Two hours tracking down Peter's Catholic Sacramental Certifications

- Ten hours to complete the Catholic workbook (*For Better & For Ever*)

- Forty hours to complete the online Catholic workshop

- Ten hours teaching Peter everything I learned in the Catholic workshop

- Two hours meeting with our Catholic priest to officiate the private ceremony

- Three hours in Zoom meetings with Reverend Willard

- One hour taking Reverend Willard's test

- One hour reading the article "Masters of Love"

- Two hours selecting readings for a Catholic ceremony and a Christian ceremony

After a total of **seventy-seven hours** of preparation, Peter and I were approved to be married privately at St. Rita's and at The Brantley Hotel with Reverend Willard. We had to be the most well-prepared couple for marriage. There would be no excuse for our marriage to fail.

Preparing for the Catholic ceremony versus the Christian ceremony differed in their approaches.

The Christian church tested our compatibility with the goal of providing us tools to use when future problems arise.

The Christian church covered topics like dealing with future in-laws, effective communication, money management, balancing careers, and other hot topics that commonly cause strife between couples. Everything we learned was practical.

The Catholic church focused less on relationship management tools and more on spirituality. We learned how God strives to prepare us to experience the gift of marriage. We learned how God directs us to find someone to share our lives with and how marriage is a celebration that represents the sacred love God has for us. We were able to understand the sanctity of marriage through scripture.

Peter and I were lucky to benefit from both approaches. We remind each other of our strengths and weaknesses, as we learned through our Christian counseling to support one another. We lean on our faith, which we enriched during our Catholic prep, by remembering God has a plan for us.

Preparing for Marriage Advice

- **Learn what marriage means for each of you.** No matter what path you take toward preparing for marriage, be receptive to learning from it. If you are not religious, I highly encourage **at least** one session of couples' therapy to learn about each other's beliefs around marriage.

- **Remember your marriage prep when it matters most.** At the end of the day, we can't rely on our parents as an example of what constitutes a happy or unhappy marriage. There is no textbook definition or recipe to create one. No one comes without faults; we can all be selfish at times. Find a way to learn how to love your partner, even when you're mad as hell.

THE BRIDAL PORTRAITS

I t hadn't occurred to me that bridal portraits could be taken at a studio in advance of the wedding. I had no intention of taking professional pictures in my gown before the wedding until my mom shared her experience.

"I took a bridal portrait at a studio in New Jersey a month before the wedding." She held up a framed photograph of her wearing her gown and veil. "This is the only decent photograph I have of me in my gown. The day of the wedding was ninety-eight degrees, my hair was frizzy, and someone stole my bra, so I looked flat chested."

I didn't argue with her. I've seen her wedding album and can confirm that her bridal party looked sweaty—and not in a natural-glow, dewy way.

I wasn't thrilled at the idea of committing an entire day for a photoshoot when the wedding was far from complete, and my work projects demanded attention. Based on my mother's advice, I hired my wedding photographer to capture a bridal portrait. Thompson Photo is a husband-and-wife team, and Bri took the lead on this project. She reserved a trendy studio in West Midtown on April eighth, one month prior to my wedding. The studio would serve as an elegant backdrop with its Parisian aesthetic, natural light, and bright white props.

Two days before the photoshoot, I booked a manicure, pedicure, and spray tan appointment. I was in the midst of testing spray tan colors; I needed to know exactly what my tan would look like on the day of my wedding. I couldn't risk a spray tan that would look unnatural, or worse, splotchy.

My pre-photoshoot routine was on track for my bridal portraits, except for my wardrobe. My gown was in desperate need of a second round of alterations, which could not be completed before my bridal portraits. I swung by Tori's Bridal and snatched my dress, promising to bring it back the very next day for final alterations.

The morning of my bridal portraits, I allotted ample time to shower, shave, and perform my pageant-style beauty routine. My mom picked me up at my apartment and drove us into the city for the photoshoot. When we arrived at the studio, we met the owner, a young, dark-haired woman, who gave us the rundown. She showed us the lighting panel, Wi-Fi password, and handed us plastic shoe covers to avoid scuffing her clean, white floors.

My mom chirped, "Wow, this place is so fancy! It looks like an apartment. You could live here!"

I paid for precisely one hour at the studio, so I got down to business and hastily changed into my heavy, beaded gown. It took my mom and Bri eight minutes to clip the tulle over-skirt to my waist, which was a painfully long time to have two people inches from my butt.

Once I was dressed and ready to go, Bri experimented with the lighting and positioned me for the first full-body shot. She stretched out my dramatic train and angled my face slightly to the left to capture my silhouette. I was standing in the center of an airy loft with twenty feet of natural light pouring onto my face. I could tell that this photo was going to be breathtaking.

Next, Bri instructed, "Look down at your gown for the next round of photos."

When I shifted my gaze downward, I noticed my veil didn't match my gown. I kept staring at my veil and eventually asked Bri, "Does this match, or am I going crazy?"

Bri walked over and verified, "Oh, yeah, that's odd! Your veil is ivory, and your gown is white!

"They must have ordered me the wrong color veil!" I shrieked.

Wanting to get in on the action, my mom scurried over in her plastic-covered sneakers to see what the fuss was about.

"Can you please call Tori's Bridal and let them know my veil is the wrong color?" I pleaded. "I have to keep taking photos, we only have the studio for thirty more minutes."

My mom called the bridal shop and was placed on hold for ten minutes until they finally connected her with Joe's assistant. "They want you to send an email with a photo of the veil next to your gown," my mom told me. "Joe's assistant warned me that they might not be able to order a custom veil in time. She said they take two to three months to order, and we are only four weeks away from the wedding."

I scoffed. "They better do something!"

"Since we have had ownership of the gown for five months now, they might not be able to give us a refund on the ivory veil either," my mother continued.

I was beyond upset with the situation, but I knew I needed to remain calm and concentrate on the task at hand—capturing a bridal portrait.

I was able to overlook my eggshell veil, but I couldn't get past the discomfort of my gown. My dress kept falling, and I was flashing the camera like a college freshman on spring break. I had to wiggle my body into the top of the gown to resituate every five minutes.

Buttercream veil aside, I was still able to take serene bridal portraits in front of a floor-length gold mirror, stretched out across a white couch, and standing near a black-and-white fireplace.

For more photos, go to
www.thecovidbridebysara.com/post/portraits

© *Willett Photo*

Bridal Portrait Advice

- **Schedule a bridal portrait!** The biggest lesson to learn from this chapter is do not skip this step of the process. While taking photos, we learned that my veil was the wrong color. This would have been unsolvable on the wedding day, but we were able to abort this crisis and order another veil in time.

- **Consider the cleanliness of your gown on your wedding day.** I loved how my bridal portraits turned out, and I admire how clean and crisp my gown looks. No one probably told you, but if you take wedding pictures outside or have an outdoor ceremony, your gown will get a little dirty. It's unavoidable, and it will continue to get dirtier as the day goes on.

- **Avoid the stress of the unknown!** Everything is unpredictable on your wedding day, and there is no way to guarantee pleasant weather, soft lighting, or the right scenery for a bridal portrait. I could rest assured knowing that I had already captured an editorial-style bridal portrait. Scheduling a specific time for portraits was stress free, **for the most part**, and I can't recommend this enough to future brides!

The Budget Bride

To save money on bridal portraits, consider styling your own hair and makeup. If you don't trust your skills, schedule your wedding day hair and makeup trial for the morning before your bridal portraits. You don't need a fancy studio; you could take photos at your house, apartment, a family member's house, or even outside if you're not worried about the bottom of your gown getting dirty.

The purpose of bridal portraits is not to add an extra expense but to give you peace of mind that you have already captured a photograph in your gown that you adore. It's one less thing to worry about on your wedding day.

THE FINAL FITTING

As promised, I returned my wedding gown to Sue at Tori's Bridal for the final round of alterations. Once complete, my final fitting would be the last opportunity to try on my gown before the wedding. Whatever it looked like on that day was as good as it was going to get.

My mom couldn't make my appointment, so I brought my aunt along with me. Like my mother, she is brutally honest and would speak up if it didn't look right.

I changed into my gown and walked toward the mirrors to show my aunt. She gasped, "It's gorgeous, Sara!"

"Really?" I questioned. "It feels a little uncomfy, but I love the way it looks." I didn't want to complain, but the final alterations failed to make the gown any more fun to wear than it had been before alterations or during my bridal portraits. It was just as heavy, itchy, and revealing, though the risk of flashing the bridal party and guests had been addressed.

Sue attempted to teach my aunt and me how to bustle the back of the gown. This was needed if I wanted to move about the ballroom without people trampling over my train. Since the train was theatrically long, Sue created a three-point contraption and asked my aunt to take a video of her securing it. If a bustle requires a video tutorial, it is too complex for my blood.

After fussing with the bustle, Sue instructed me to turn around and look at it. I did my best not to burst out laughing when I caught a glimpse of the side view. I looked like I had a poufy tail! I loathed the way it looked, but I couldn't avoid it if I wanted to move freely during the reception. I had a sudden horrible realization that I couldn't wear my gown all night. Now that it was skintight, it was impossible to sit in.

My aunt and I left the appointment with my wedding gown in hand.

When I returned home, my mom was in the kitchen prepping dinner. I marched in and announced, "I can't wear this gown all night." I held the heavy garment bag above my head. "It's even more miserable now that it's been altered!"

"You need to find another dress for the reception, then. You can't wear your Mac Duggal dress for the rest of the night; it's not a wedding gown. I can't believe you bought an uncomfortable dress," she stated with a sigh of irritation.

It was a month before the wedding, and I had to find a second wedding gown STAT!

THE SECOND
WEDDING GOWN

I had a wedding gown that felt like a Kardashian-style waist trainer and a nonrefundable Mac Duggal first-dance dress that wasn't formal **or bridal** enough for my reception.

"I didn't realize you couldn't dance at all in your wedding gown," my mom scolded me again. "I thought you just couldn't do your first dance in that gown."

Equally upset, I shot back with, "I truly thought that if it was altered to fit my body, it would be okay. Now it's just tight and makes me look like a Victorian woman from the nineteenth century when it's bustled! Tell me I don't look like this?" I showed her Google images of "Bustle Era" on my phone.

In four short weeks, I'd be walking down the aisle in a gown that was intolerable. I'd be able to get out of it for our first dance, before spending the rest of the reception weighed down and unable to sit or dance. Just when I began to feel sorry for myself, my wedding planner, Margot, texted me.

Margot: *How was your final fitting?*
Sara: *Not great...*

Margot: *Do you want me to call my friend at Luxe Bridal? She might be able to sell you a sample gown from her latest trunk show. www.luxebridalatl.com*

I clicked on the link and read the business hours. "Thursday: 11:00 a.m. to 7:00 p.m." It was only 4:30 p.m., and I could be there by 6:00 p.m. if I left right away. Finding another gown became an urgent matter, so I was willing to face my hatred for commuting to the city during rush hour.

Sara: *Sure!! Let me know ASAP!! I could be there by 6:00 p.m.*

Margot confirmed my appointment, and I headed out the door, alone.

"Facetime me if you find anything you like!" my mom yelled after me.

On my commute toward the city, I called Vivienne, my maid of honor, to fill her in on my wedding dress drama.

"I'll meet you there! I'm only twenty minutes from Buckhead," Vivienne offered, no questions asked. She didn't even try to talk me out of wasting money on a third gown. She knew it was a serious dilemma if I was willing to commute to the city by myself to try on sample gowns.

Vivienne waited in the parking lot for me to arrive, and we entered the shop together. Luxe Bridal was the most exquisite shop I had ever seen. It honored its French name with opulent Parisian décor, high ceilings, crystal chandeliers, and tall gold clothing racks overflowing with vogue haute-couture gowns. Luxe Bridal carried international designers from Lebanon, Spain, Italy, and Israel whose names I stumbled over.

Surrounded by racks of lace, sequins, sparkles, beads, feathers, and flowers, I thought, *if I don't find a gown here, I won't find one anywhere.*

The owner of the boutique introduced herself to us. "Hi, ladies. My name is Shaya. Margot told me that I would be expecting you today."

Vivienne and I introduced ourselves and described what had happened with my first wedding gown.

"I feel terrible about your situation. Would you rather bring it in to our expert seamstress?" she offered. "She can fix it for you. We can add an illusion neckline or straps? Whatever is easiest for you...I want to be part of the solution."

Shaya was a striking young businesswoman, marginally over the age of thirty, who was clearly hustling us. I read a sales and negotiations book years ago and recognized her approach. Offering a prospective client a lesser solution makes your high-ticket solution more desirable. In the nicest way, Shaya was saying, "Our product is outside your price range, but we still want to help you with your problem." Her subtle way of not pushing a sale only made me want one of her gowns more!

"I have my heart set on finding a new gown. I've altered my current gown twice, and I can't risk another round of alterations this close to the wedding. Plus, what makes it uncomfortable also makes it beautiful. Adding straps or cutting off the train would take away its wow factor," I rationalized.

Once Shaya knew I was committed to buying a gown, she and her three sales associates in little black dresses started to carry designer gowns into the dressing room. I stopped one of the sales associates, "I think that gown is too much for me! It needs to be as light as a nightgown. Don't get me wrong, it's stunning, but I need something simple."

I cycled through the gowns but kept going back to the first one that caught my eye, a soft ivory gown from an Israeli designer. Underneath the buttery-soft tulle skirt was a lining of sequins leading up to a structured bodice that hugged my hips. There were delicate spaghetti straps that matched the back of the gown's lace-up corset string. It fit all of my specifications—it was lightweight, flowy, and fit me like a glove without a single alteration needed.

Eventually, I Facetimed my mom from the poorly lit fitting room to show her the gown.

"How much is it?" my mom asked indifferently. The lighting and poor cellular service did not do the gown justice.

I shouted into my phone, "I'll let you know soon. The owner has to ask the designer if it's all right to sell the sample gown. The designer lives in Israel, so hopefully she responds soon."

Saying that out loud made me realize Shaya's second sales tactic—pretending to offer a special price and sale. I got dressed and met Shaya at the counter. "I'm going to grab a coffee from Starbucks. Here is my number." I scribbled it on a sticky note. "Call me when you know the price." I left before she could negotiate further.

Minutes later, I received a text message from one of the sales associates.

Luxe Bridal: The gown is $6,400, but we can sell it at a 15% discount because it's a sample.

I opened the calculator app on my phone and calculated a fifteen percent discount plus a seven-point-five percent sales tax, bringing the final price of the gown to $5,848. That was a lot of money to pay for a sample gown that had been tried on multiple times.

Sara: Hi, thank you. Could I show my mom the dress tomorrow morning before deciding?

Luxe Bridal: Yes. Shaya can meet you at her warehouse in Newnan at 11:00 a.m.

I drove back home to Peachtree City to eat the plate of dinner my parents set aside for me. I discussed the gown with my parents and explained how Shaya was charging too high a price for a sample gown.

"What do you want to offer for the gown?" my dad asked.

"The max I would be willing to spend is five thousand dollars," I shared.

Right then and there, my dad cut me a check to Luxe Bridal for $5,000 and hollered, "Go get 'em, Tiger!"

The next morning, my mom and I drove together to Shaya's warehouse in Newnan. We made our way to the door and noticed it was locked. "I thought we confirmed meeting at eleven." I was puzzled. "Let me try calling her."

I called Shaya's cell phone number, but it went straight to voicemail. I called the store number and got no answer. I called the sales associate who texted me the day before, and her mailbox was full. Finally, I sent a text message to the sales associate.

> **Sara:** Hi, sorry to bother you. We are at the warehouse, and the doors are locked.

We stood at the door for another seven minutes until I got a response that Shaya was on her way.

Forty-five minutes later, Shaya pulled up to the warehouse in a Ford F250 truck and hopped out of the driver's seat wearing a black lady suit and pink Prada pumps. She opened the door to the warehouse and offered, "Look around and see if you find anything. These samples are going to be discounted more because they are 2018–2019 designs."

I was intrigued by the warehouse of sample gowns but dumbfounded by what was happening. I thought she was bringing the gown I liked to her warehouse so I could show my mom. We had already been waiting an hour, and she didn't have the gown I wanted. This was just another sales tactic—the longer we invested our time into finding a gown, the more likely we would want to purchase a gown.

"Do you have the gown I tried on yesterday? I wanted to show my mom **that** gown," I reminded Shaya.

"I completely forgot! Let me have one of my sales associates drive it over now!" Shaya insisted.

Now we were really burning daylight. It would take an hour for a sales associate to drive the dress to the warehouse from Buckhead.

"Okay, thanks! We're going to grab lunch in the meantime. Give me a call when it gets here." I did my best not to sound aggravated.

By the time we had lunch and came back, the gown was waiting for me. I humored my mother and tried on a couple of other sample gowns but saved my favorite gown for last. I strutted out of the dressing room; my mom was breathless. "You look like a princess! How romantic and whimsical."

Ahhh! I could hear angels singing from above. I got the approval from my mom! It was time to close the deal.

"How much?" I asked Shaya like I didn't already know.

"The best I can do is fifty-four hundred dollars cash or check. This gown is in exceptional condition and from the new Spring 2021 collection," Shaya justified.

Sticking to my guns, I insisted, "The best I can do is five thousand dollars."

My mom folded like a losing poker hand despite being warned that Shaya was a master saleswoman. "Sara, why don't you Venmo her for the rest of the gown?" she objected.

I headed into the dressing room to change back into my yoga biker shorts and old Led Zeppelin t-shirt. I strolled out of the dressing room holding the $5,000 check in my hand and looked Shaya in the eyes. I repeated, "This is the best I can do, but I'd be happy to film some marketing videos for you to make up the difference."

Shaya's expression softened, and she congratulated me, "Take this as my wedding gift to you."

I tried my best not to smile too big while thanking her again and again for the gown. We scheduled a time for me to film content that week. My mom and I drove home with our prize in hand, and I began brainstorming ways to pay my dad back for this dress.

"Oh! I have an idea!" My mom shouted. "Why don't you sell your old gowns?"

"That's a great idea! I'm going to do that right when we get home." My gowns were as good as new because I had only worn most of them once for either a gala, formal, prom, or pageant.

The rest of my afternoon was dedicated to setting up an account on Tradesy and Poshmark, both secondhand e-commerce websites, to sell my gowns.

I took front, side, and back view photographs of twenty gowns. Next, I identified each like a biologist with a new species using the seven main taxonomic ranks (kingdom, phylum, etc.), except my classifications were designer, size, color, material, condition, original price, and sale price. Needless to say, after all of this effort, I only made one sale for a whopping fifty bucks. I handed my dad fifty dollars cash and told him I would need a little time to collect the rest.

Additional Wedding Gown Advice

- **Buy the right gown the first time!** Learn from my mistake. I want to encourage brides to select a wedding gown that they don't just see themselves getting married in, but a gown they can wear the **entire** night. To avoid making the mistakes that I did, ask yourself:

- Will this gown be difficult to dance in?
- Will this gown be hard to eat in?
- Can I sit comfortably in this gown?
- If I die tomorrow, do I want to be buried in this gown?

If you can candidly answer each of those questions and have zero reservations about your choice of gown, then go for it!

THE SEATING CHART

Believe me when I tell you, the seating chart is one of the most exasperating aspects of wedding planning. Before 2020, brides didn't have a global pandemic to add to the mix, making the entire process even more tedious.

The trend today is a seating chart board that lists every table and guest. In my opinion, it looks more like a train schedule than a seating chart. At a wedding I recently attended, I stood in front of the seating chart board far too long, squinting my eyes. I couldn't find my name because guests weren't listed in alphabetical order. It makes sense; how weird would it be to sit at a table with folks, and the only common denominator is the first letter of your last name?

Once you locate your name on the board, you make your way to the table to find your seat indicated by a name card placed at each chair. This sought-after board method was not practical for my large guest list, and I lacked the desire to assign seats like a kindergarten teacher.

find your table

SARA + PETER

MAY 8, 2021

TABLE 1
Amara Austin
Opal Callahan
Mason Brown
Ridley MacArthur
Esther Germanson

TABLE 2
Mason Mathis
Averi Montgomery
Kaya Garza
Melanie Compton
Mikayla Torres

TABLE 3
Abraham Watson
Terrell Beal
Joshua Silva
Mazely Haeler
Dana Stuart

TABLE 4
India Roach
Ezequiel Wolf
Kristina Rodgers
Finn Lewis
Genna Preston

TABLE 5
Dana Stuart
Angel Powers
Anton Reilly
Diamond Bedford
Malaya Jefferson

TABLE 6
Edyn Ginn
Gabriella Shaffer
Mikail Thorpe
Trey Compton

TABLE 7
Khalil Garza
Julianna Arroyo
Jennifer Gilmore
Abigail Rogers
Xiomara Rios

TABLE 8
Amara Austin
Opal Callahan
Mason Brown
Ridley MacArthur
Esther Germanson

TABLE 9
Destiny Cross
Kelly Townsend
Abraham Watson
Terrell Beal

TABLE 10
Amara Austin
Opal Callahan
Mason Brown
Ridley MacArthur
Esther Germanson

TABLE 11
Amara Austin
Opal Callahan
Mason Brown
Ridley MacArthur
Esther Germanson

TABLE 12
Jason Wilks
Mason Mathis
Averi Montgomery
Kaya Garza
Melanie Compton

TABLE 13
Dana Stuart
Angel Powers
Anton Reilly
Diamond Bedford
Malaya Jefferson

TABLE 14
Edyn Ginn
Gabriella Shaffer
Mikail Thorpe
Trey Compton

TABLE 15
Khalil Garza
Julianna Arroyo
Jennifer Gilmore
Abigail Rogers
Xiomara Rios

TABLE 16
Amara Austin
Opal Callahan
Mason Brown
Ridley MacArthur
Esther Germanson

TABLE 17
Destiny Cross
Kelly Townsend
Abraham Watson
Terrell Beal

TABLE 18
Amara Austin
Opal Callahan
Mason Brown
Ridley MacArthur
Esther Germanson

TABLE 19
Amara Austin
Opal Callahan
Mason Brown
Ridley MacArthur
Esther Germanson

TABLE 20
Jazmyn Scott
Asma Ginn
Daniel Spence
Eden Lucas

TABLE 21
Amara Austin
Opal Callahan
Mason Brown
Ridley MacArthur
Esther Germanson

TABLE 22
Amara Austin
Opal Callahan
Mason Brown
Ridley MacArthur
Esther Germanson

TABLE 23
Duncan Calderon
Jaedyn Maxwell
Julianna Doss
Jazmin Stein
Bruno Mayo

On an hour-long Zoom call with Heather from Cotton Lilies, I illustrated how I wanted to assign tables while giving my guests the freedom to choose where to sit at the table. With this in mind, Heather and I went back and forth on the best way to assign tables. We landed on the classic escort card option, listing name, table number, and entrée. We came up with a color key for the five different dinner options available; we chose gold cards for steak, blush for chicken, ivory for seafood, silver for vegetarian, and white with blush for the kids' meal.

Concluding the Zoom meeting, Heather said, "I am going to need your final guest list by next Friday." That was three weeks before the wedding.

"Alrighty." I nodded, knowing I had to follow up with a handful of guests.

"Make sure you format the list in an Excel spreadsheet in alphabetical order. The first column should be the names how you want them printed, second column table number, and third column entree." Heather spoke with her hands.

Acting like I had already had it done, I replied, "Not a problem." In reality, we didn't have a final guest count, I hadn't assigned table numbers, and plus-ones were listed as "so and so's girlfriend?"

Heather and I wrapped up the meeting with me promising her a list by the end of the week.

The Tables

The next afternoon, I met my mom at her house to begin assembling the seating chart. Pierre, our venue coordinator at The Brantley Hotel, emailed a ballroom floor plan specific to our event. I had it printed large enough to spread across my mother's kitchen table and brought a couple standard-size copies for drafts.

I unrolled the floor plan like a treasure map and stared at it. In the center of the ballroom, a large square represented the twenty-by-twenty-foot dance floor. In front of the dance floor, a rectangle outlined the stage. Opposite the stage, two long rectangles formed the head table. On the right and left of the dance floor, circles indicated the tables numbered one through twenty-three.

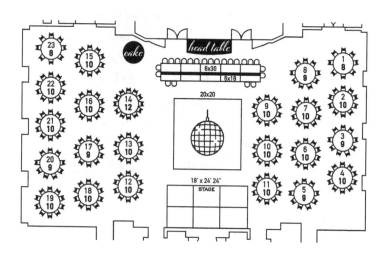

Overwhelmed by the task at hand, I asked, "Mom, do you have any colored pencils?"

"Sure, right in here." My mom opened a drawer designated to junk, unidentifiable cords, and my mom's calendar. She pulled out a box of colored pencils and handed them to me. I removed a pink pencil and a blue pencil. "I think the first thing we need to do is divide the tables between our side and Peter's side." I held up the pink and blue pencils.

My mom agreed we should divide the tables between the families before deciding who sits at them. This task was easier said than done. It took three rounds of color mapping the ballroom before we were content with the plans.

In the first attempt at dividing the tables, I simply alternated pink, blue, pink, blue until each circle was colored. We reviewed the finished map and realized that all of the tables with the best location overlooking the dance floor were pink. We agreed this wasn't fair, and we needed to give up some of our prime real estate.

I crumpled up the floor plan copy and took another stab at it. On the second attempt, we accidentally segregated the guest list; the left side of the ballroom was overwhelmingly pink, and the right side of the ballroom was overwhelmingly blue.

I crumpled up that floor plan and tried again. Finally, we were able to balance the ballroom map between blue circles and pink circles without favoring either color to one side of the room.

"Third time's the charm!" I cheered. Now that my mom and I had accomplished mapping out the ballroom, we would begin placing guests into groups of ten on an entirely new day. We'd had enough wedding planning for one afternoon!

The Planning Pizza Party

Three days later, I invited Vivienne and mom to my apartment for a seating chart pizza party. I was pressed to complete this because the final list was due to Heather in a couple of days.

To prepare for our meeting, I tidied up my apartment and placed an order at my favorite pizzeria. I printed three copies of the confirmed RSVP list and three copies of the pink and blue ballroom floor plan.

It was like pulling teeth to get guests to RSVP! Since our wedding RSVP cards were being held captive with our ex-wedding planner, we had to remind guests to RSVP **again**, but online. On top of our missing cards, our invitations listed the incorrect due date, stringing out responses from procrastinators who were still reluctant to commit to a wedding during COVID. We had a total of two hundred and fifty confirmed guests, fifty-three no's and **twenty-four pending** RSVPs.

The missing responses fell into two categories, my dad's friends and Peter's invites. I was more forgiving of Peter's invites because they would be traveling from Los Angeles, where the lockdowns were more stringent. Plus, none of Peter's friends knew me because we got engaged at the dawn of the pandemic, so why would they risk their lives for **my** wedding?

Regardless of the reason behind the missing RSVPs, I needed a final headcount for Heather, the hotel, and other vendors from whom we rented chairs, linens, flatware, glasses, plates, and more. Depending on our headcount, our final invoice from each vendor could drastically change. I was already over budget and didn't want to pay for any extras for guests who weren't coming.

Thirty minutes before our pizza and seating chart session, I called my dad to remind him of his outstanding RSVPs.

"Hey there, Sara Belle," my dad answered. "What's going on?"

"Hi, I was curious if you ever heard back from the list of people I texted you yesterday morning?" I tried my best not to sound nagging.

"Well, Bob and Terry are coming." My dad already sounded annoyed. "They told me."

"Okay, well, I never got a formal RSVP from them. How do I know what they want to eat?" I asked.

"Give them one steak and one chicken," my dad said seriously.

"Okay, I guess I can do that," I replied. "It just doesn't feel like a solid RSVP."

"What do you want me to do? They told me they were coming. I can't ask them again. I'm sorry they didn't RSVP properly." My dad was clearly frustrated with this process.

Tiptoeing with my voice, I said, "It's okay. What about the other names?"

"Sara, I have left all of them voicemails, and I haven't heard back yet. I can't call them again. Just put them down as coming and move on." My dad ended the conversation.

I felt terrible about the possibility of spending money on guests that wouldn't come but also aggravated that I would have to update the seating chart if they RSVPed no.

I texted Peter with the list of his outstanding RSVPs and asked if he could get an answer quickly.

Peter responded: *Sure, I can do this after work.*

My mom, the pizzas, and my first mental breakdown of the evening showed up all at the same time. "Mom, how can these people be so rude to leave us hanging with no RSVP three weeks before the wedding? You know by now if you can come or not! You also know if you don't want to come because of COVID!"

"I agree," my mom said. "I think it's rude that these people haven't responded by now."

"Peter has fourteen guests who haven't RSVPed either," I complained. "I need those responses **now**."

"When is he going to give them to you?" my mom asked while serving herself a hot piece of pizza.

"When he gets home, he said. That's too late. Let's just cancel the meeting tonight and do it when we get the last of the RSVPs." I felt utterly defeated.

I texted Vivienne to cancel our meeting: *Hey Viv, I'm sorry to do this so last minute, but don't bother coming over tonight. We still don't have an RSVP from 24 guests.*

Vivienne knows how to handle my overly dramatic mood swings. Instead of sending a passive-aggressive text like "ok." or "I'm 2 mins away and just sat in 45 mins of traffic," she sent: *Okay, I'm close by and going to run to Publix to pick up some things. Let me know if you change your mind.*

Fifteen minutes passed as I ate three pieces of pizza and came to my senses.

Sara: *Do you still want to come over and put together the seating chart? We can work with what we have!*

Vivienne: *Be there in 5*

This is just one example of how Vivienne is the best friend a girl could ask for. She arrived within minutes, and the three of us began to discuss a strategy for going about grouping guests together.

We unanimously agreed that we should begin by grouping guests into lists of ten before deciding which pink table to place them at. After trial and error attempting to format the tables into an Excel document, I grabbed twenty-six blank sheets of printer paper and wrote the numbers one through ten down the left-hand side. One by one, we went through the list and began pairing people together.

We took our time separating family members we knew would fight. We discussed the personalities of my friends and tried to group people who would hit it off. We even tried matchmaking by placing my single friends at a table with one or two single bachelors. From six to eight-thirty, the three of us assembled and plotted tables. Peter walked in the door from work while we were finishing my side of the guest list.

"Peter, come help us with the seating chart for your tables," I called toward the door, demanding his help before he could even place his briefcase on the floor.

Peter moseyed over to the kitchen island with pages of printer paper scattered across the counter and said, "You know I could have figured out a formula in Excel to automatically format this for you, right?"

I exploded with my second meltdown of the evening. "We tried to do it in Excel first, but we couldn't visualize the tables. This has been quick and straightforward, and we've been able to shift people around easily."

"Geez, I'm just trying to help," Peter defended himself.

"Okay, well, that's not helping because we have been doing this for hours, and you're finally here. Why don't you help us put together **your** list of tables?" I barked at him.

Peter sat down at my computer and started making his list in Excel, only to end up switching to the paper and pen method as well. He never would admit it was easier, but it didn't matter if it was getting done. Over the next two hours, Vivienne and Peter finalized his seating chart on paper and then transitioned handwritten documents into the Excel format Heather requested. My mom and I lost interest after a while, so she scrolled through Instagram while I lay on the couch to avoid inserting my opinion.

Once the spreadsheet was complete, we emailed it to Heather. Over the next three weeks, I received numerous regrets and changed RSVP responses. Of course, it was too late for Heather to adjust what she sent to the printer.

Every time I received another 'no,' I sent The Brantley Hotel an updated table overview, removing a chair or two from the floor plan. Unfortunately, it was also too late to get my money back for each plated dinner and premium cocktail package, but at least I could update the number of chairs per table up to five days before the wedding. No one wants to sit at a table with a bunch of empty chairs!

Seating Chart Advice

- **Spend time making a seating chart!** It is time-consuming to think through the best way to orient your guests, but it allows you to mix your family and friends in a way that will create energy and interest. Giving assigned tables ensures that everyone has a home base for the night. It eliminates the rush of guests into the ballroom to stake their territory; family members don't have to worry about whether or not they can snag a seat near the bride or groom. In my opinion, grandparents deserve the best seats in the house! Assigned tables make it possible for women to stash their stylish yet agonizing stilettos under their table and slip away to the dance floor.

- **Intermix the bride's and groom's guests throughout the room.** I'm **not** endorsing blending the tables, but you also don't want to isolate the bride's or groom's guests to one area of the room. The way I divided the ballroom floor plan by alternating between a table for the bride and a table for the groom actually enhanced our reception mingling. I was able to meet Peter's guests because I would be passing them on my way to greet my friends! If my friends were isolated to one side of the room, I would be less inclined to explore the other half of the ballroom.

- **Don't sweat it!** If the seating arrangements don't turn out the day of your wedding, just roll with it!

The Budget Bride

When making your seating chart, make sure to note who is under twenty-one and who won't be drinking (whether it be religious or health reasons). By making detailed notes on your seating chart document for your venue, you can save hundreds of dollars on alcohol expenses for every youth or pregnant woman! There is no point in paying for an alcohol package for people who won't be consuming. Also, make your RSVP deadline before the three-week mark to save money on unnecessary rentals. If you invite three hundred guests and only two hundred and fifty RSVP yes, you still have time to cut chairs, napkins, linens, glassware, and even cake!

THE FINAL DETAILS

Consumed with the seating chart, the status of the other stationery items slipped my mind. After relocating the reception to The Brantley Hotel, I was over budget and needed to scale back on nonessential details. Back in November, I discussed a number of ancillary accents with Heather, my stationer. I was glad she had encouraged me to wait until closer to the wedding date to order any extras because **a lot** had changed. I emailed Heather to ask for a quote and planned on eliminating the custom boxes of gold matches, monogrammed cocktail stirrers, and gold-pressed cocktail napkins.

A week went by, and I hadn't heard back. I assumed she was drowning in the wedding season because April is the most desirable month for weddings in Georgia. I sent **another** email to remind her I needed a quote. I could no longer justify spending money on keepsakes—something that felt vital at the time now became irrelevant. Finally, she emailed me back.

To: Sara La Chapelle
From: Heather Cotton Lilies
Date: Monday, April 12, 2021, 2:39 p.m. EST
Subject: RE: Quote for Stationery Extras

Hi Sara

I have time blocked off to design the rest of your items
next week. I've already ordered the napkins, cocktail
stirrers and matches so we're ready to go on those.

Thank you!
Heather

I began to panic at her response. I never approved those
items going to print! I quickly responded, asking if she could
cancel the order. A few days later, she emailed me again.

To: Sara La Chapelle
From: Heather Cotton Lilies
Date: Thursday, April 15, 2021, 12:32 p.m. EST

Hello,

It is too late to cancel the items, but I can give them to
you with an 18% discount or recycle them. Let me know.
I am also missing information:

1. Program songs for various parts in the wedding
2. Words of thanks for back of wedding program
3. Vegetarian menu entree
4. Bar menu verbiage
5. Final decision of signs

Heather

I couldn't stand the idea of Heather throwing away unused party supplies, so I ended up agreeing to the discounted price. Her email reminded me that I had yet to confirm the ceremony music.

As a wedding gift, Vivienne hooked me up with Gilbert Music through her father's connections with the Atlanta symphony. I hired a string trio to accompany a vocal soloist, my distant cousin Jeff. Jeff is from the non-Italian side of my family, so I am not sure if I barely know him or if there were just normal family boundaries between us growing up. Jeff has an astounding voice that landed him a college scholarship, and I was honored to have him perform at the ceremony.

I sent an email to Jeff and Gilbert Music to make sure I was correctly listing the ceremony songs we agreed to. I wanted them to play "The Prayer" for the seating of the parents and "Ave Maria" for the bridal party's arrival. I got a response from Gilbert Music right away.

To: Sara; Jeff
From: Gilbert Music
Date: Friday, April 16, 2021, 12:14 p.m. EST
Subject: Re: La Chapelle Wedding Music

Hi Sara,

Yes, we can play it in that order. Have you decided what you are going to walk down the aisle to? We can play almost anything from the Beatles, Christina Perri, to Ed Sheeran.

Gilbert

My first instinct was to walk down the aisle to a contemporary song, so I opened my Spotify Love Songs playlist for inspiration. Nothing was jumping out at me. After a year of planning a wedding during COVID, I had become numb to music. With the lack of emotional pull toward any one song, I opted for the traditional "Wedding March" by Mendelssohn and "The Arrival of the Queen of Sheba" by Handel. My ceremony program information was nearly complete.

I formatted an Excel spreadsheet with the dinner and bar menu information and sent them to Heather. A week later, her design proofs hit my inbox. I printed them out, grabbed a highlighter, and reviewed each document with a fine-tooth comb. I found little typos and one **big mistake.**

Heather designed four separate menus for each entree instead of one universal menu. She forgot that we were not assigning seats, just tables. It wouldn't be possible to set four different menus at the tables if we didn't know who would sit where, and with what entree. I emailed her the corrections and asked if she could design one menu that listed all possible entree options: pan roasted beef filet, pan seared southern bass, smoked chicken supreme, black peppercorn gnocchi, and the children's bento box.

Because Cotton Lilies produced the bulk of our wedding accessories, I made a list of everything we'd ordered so I could confirm receipt of items. In the wedding workshop, I labeled a large clear storage bin with the purchase order, expecting to organize the items myself. Unfortunately, I had no more availability to swing by Cotton Lilies in Atlanta because my schedule was bombarded with last-minute tasks. Margot volunteered to retrieve the paper goods, event signage, and monogrammed extras.

With the amount of funds and time I devoted to personalizing our wedding, I figured the stationery items would be well worth it. However, I made the mistake of not reviewing these before the wedding weekend, so I wouldn't find out things were missing until later.

THE GRAND SEND-OFF

Time was dwindling away before the big day. Three and a half weeks before the wedding, Peter and I still hadn't nailed down our grand exit. You know, that moment at the end of the night when the guests gather around to see the new happy couple escape in their tacky getaway car while they fervently wave goodbye to family and friends?

If you have attended a wedding in the past decade, you probably associate this tradition with a pack of matches and a bucket of sparklers. The sparkler trend has continued to dominate wedding exits for many years—it looks magical in photos! But if I am being completely frank, I am **over this** trend!

The past few weddings I've attended, I've noticed that lighting the sparklers never happens in unison. The front of the send-off line lights their sparklers first, but the three minutes it takes to transfer the spark to the end of the line, the first of the sparklers are burned out. The front of the line is left waving around what remains of the sparkler—a bent, burnt wire. I may also have a stronger revulsion to the sparkler send-off because I have a deep fear of drunk people in possession of fire. Visions of hair catching fire or gowns going up in flames burn in my mind. I've actually been to a wedding where somebody's great aunt's hair caught on fire! Could you imagine?

© *Neal Reeves*

Our venue change limited what Peter and I could arrange for our grand sendoff. The only thing I had solidified was reserving a 1961 white Austin Princess Rolls-Royce limousine with a complimentary bottle of champagne and a glass divider–*wink, wink.*

Way back at the genesis of our wedding planning adventure, we arranged for a display of fireworks in the front courtyard at Braxton Country Club. It had been a struggle to get the club to agree to fireworks, but the right amount of Southern charm goes a long way. Guests would gather under the patio to watch a fireworks show, then catch an elevated glimpse of Peter and me leaving in our old-fashioned getaway car.

When we changed venues, we had to start from scratch. Naturally, the hotel immediately vetoed the fireworks show. Seeking advice, I called Margot.

"Because the ballroom is on the fourth floor of the hotel, there are only two viable options," Margot explained. "The first option would be to do an indoor exit. The guests could line up down the grand staircase and throw rose petals. Here's the catch...there's a fifteen hundred dollar clean-up fee if you throw anything."

"Fifteen hundred dollars!?" I squealed. "How quick can I sell an organ? What's the other option?"

"The second option is an outdoor exit," she continued. "I can escort guests upstairs to the fifth-floor terrace. I'm sending you a photo of another couple doing this at the hotel."

I reviewed the photo of a bride and groom kissing at the end of a long line of sparklers, complete with the city skyline in the background—a true magazine moment.

"The couple staged a fake farewell on the rooftop?" I observed.

"I guess so," Margot said.

I hated this idea for our grand exit. There was no way Margot would be able to herd two hundred and fifty tipsy wedding attendees upstairs and line them up like cattle at an auction. This was a horrendous idea; it would take people further away from the door. And it included the sparklers I'd been so keen to avoid.

Not loving either option, I mumbled, "Let's keep brainstorming."

We needed a memorable sendoff, but I refused to have a fake exit with sparklers on the fifth-floor terrace. Like every other aspect of planning my wedding, I didn't settle, but I agreed that an indoor exit down the grand staircase logistically made the most sense. I scribbled down a list of every idea, good or bad, that came to mind.

What about a bubble exit? Mmm...that would be complicated to capture in photos. Oh, I know! What if our guests waved mini flags or glow sticks? That way, we wouldn't get charged a cleanup fee. Glow sticks? No, that's tacky. Okay, I got it! What about gold and white pom-poms for team S&P? No, not the glam look I'm aiming for.

Then, I came across something that really fascinated me... the cold sparkler. A cold sparkler is a freestanding machine that looks like a small black stereo from the early 2000s. It emits bright flames that are anywhere from six to eight feet tall. It's a safe alternative to fireworks because you can't get burned—it's a cold flame. I found a company in Atlanta that leases them, but ultimately determined it would be too much to rent ample machines to line the staircase.

Later that week, I was babbling to my dad about how the grand send-off was a debacle. "It's too bad we can't just throw rose petals."

"Why not?" he asked.

"There's a fifteen-hundred-dollar cleanup fee if we throw anything." Since I was grossly over budget, I didn't consider it an option.

"At this point, what is an extra fifteen hundred dollars? You should do it; it would be epic." My dad sounded enthused by the idea.

"Really?" I couldn't believe he was on board with this, but it was just the kind of validation I needed.

All along, I was looking for a classy and romantic rose petal sendoff. I would feel like Vivien Leigh starring in a black and white film. Without further consideration, I browsed the internet for companies that sold rose petals for weddings. I pinpointed one based out of New York that sells only flower petals: Petals Plus. Their website was outdated and annoying to navigate, leading me to call their customer service number.

I was pleasantly surprised when I heard a human voice on the other line saying, "Hi, this is Amanda with Petals Plus! How can I help you?"

"Hi, Amanda, my name is Sara La Chapelle. I found your website, and I have a couple of questions. I am getting married in **three weeks**. If I were to place an order, would it be here in time? I would ideally like to have it in my hands within a week."

"I don't see that being a problem. What items are you looking at?" Amanda asked.

"I think the silk ivory rose petals."

"Yes. It looks like we have plenty of those in stock!"

"Fantastic," I said. "Okay, my next question: how many do you think I would need? I have two hundred and fifty guests, and I want everyone to throw two large handfuls of petals."

"That's a tricky question," Amanda replied. "I would say at least sixteen thousand petals to be safe. I can get you a great deal on a bulk purchase."

"How much would it be for sixteen thousand petals?" I asked, bracing for the total.

"Let me sum that up for you..." She paused for a moment. "For sixteen thousand silk rose petals, that will be three hundred and seventeen dollars."

"Three hundred and seventeen dollars!" I shouted.

"Yes." Amanda replied, not knowing where the conversation was going.

"That is the cheapest thing I have yet to buy for this wedding!" I exclaimed. "Let's do it!"

It was the best day of wedding planning yet. I ordered two hundred and fifty sheer bags and thousands of rose petals for my grand exit.

My mom was the one to individually stuff each bag with rose petals. When she was done, she carried them upstairs to store them in the wedding workshop. With only two weeks before the big day, the wedding workshop was crowded with plastic containers labeled with all of our wedding details, party favors, and welcome gifts.

While I was crossing the grand exit off my to-do list, I remembered my cold sparkler idea. *Is it still possible to include them?* Instead of the sparklers being the main attraction, I could position two machines outside behind the Rolls-Royce for a dramatic touch. I sent an email to GA Special FX to see if any were still available. If I didn't hear back within the next day or so, I would let go of the idea.

Within seconds, my phone rang with a number I didn't recognize. Unlike me, I answered. It was a sales rep from GA Special FX. Without considering my budget (or lack thereof), I ordered two cold sparklers after learning they could be positioned outside in the valet line at The Brantley Hotel.

Peter and I went from having no grand exit to having a sensational old-Hollywood style getaway.

Grand Send-off Advice

- **Make the start of your new beginning count!** There are so many ideas for grand exits that can work depending on the location of your wedding. If you get married at the beach, you can have a boat pick you up in lieu of a car. If you prefer something more regal, a horse and carriage can take you away. Find a way to end the evening in a way that will serve as your wedding's final chapter while being precious enough to be the opening scene in your new novel, the adventure of married life.

- **Don't go over budget for your send-off.** I know what you're thinking...I irresponsibly spent money on a grand exit, and you're right. I don't recommend doing this. I had no money left from my wedding budget to put toward a new pair of socks if I wanted.

The Budget Bride

Not every grand exit idea is pricey, unless, of course, you must have a horse and buggy exit. Some ideas that are budget-friendly include throwing dried flowers, colorful confetti, or releasing white balloons or lanterns. Other ideas include waving cheer poms or ribbon wands, blowing bubbles, and tossing sprinkles or dried lavender.

THE WEDDING
SCHEDULE

Having a detailed wedding schedule was the only thing
that kept me sane through the entire wedding weekend.
My bridesmaids kept asking, "Sara, are you on Xanax?!" I
was not on drugs, but I was calm and unbothered because I'd
already mapped out my every move from Thursday morning
to Tuesday evening.

A wedding schedule keeps your vendors, parents, wedding
party, guests, and yourself on time and accountable. Each
person involved has a different yet crucial role to play. If a
clear outline of the weekend is not provided, the bride and
groom will be bombarded with thousands of text messages
asking questions like: What's the address? What time do you
need me there? What time does the bus pick us up?

We canceled the church ceremony the second Reverend
Willard agreed to officiate at the hotel, creating a scheduling
nightmare. In what felt entirely last-minute to me, I emailed
my family and friends a detailed schedule with a mere seven

days until the wedding. I wanted to share it sooner, but I was in purgatory, waiting to hear whether or not The Brantley Hotel would grant us access to the venue on Friday.

The hotel couldn't guarantee access on Friday before the wedding until one week before the event. The only way to guarantee access in advance would have been to reserve the space for another $30,000. I was sitting on pins and needles waiting for the go-ahead! Without entry the day before, our bridal party wouldn't be able to rehearse the ceremony on-site, and our vendors would be forced to start setting up the wedding at 4:00 a.m. on Saturday.

By the grace of God, Pierre, the hotel event coordinator, gave us the go-ahead, enabling Margot and I to finalize the wedding timeline. Victory was ours! Having access on Friday was key because of our extensive vendor list. We'd hired over **thirty-five vendors**, which is unheard of for a single event. Our wedding was a circus compared to conventional weddings that require somewhere between six to twelve vendors. In response to our last-minute change from the church to the hotel, I had no other choice but to scrounge together wedding supplies from random resources. For instance, Margot found a retired construction worker named Karl to build a white stage for the ceremony. Karl was a stranger with no web presence, portfolio, or contract to review, but I sent him a check in the mail anyway. Across the board, our rental needs were doubled as we hired vendors to provide what Grace Christian Church would have provided, from chairs to microphones.

An Overview of the Weekend:

Our wedding weekend had back-to-back events leading up to, and following, a wedding that required intense planning to execute without fault.

Thursday—I scheduled a photoshoot of the wedding details, followed by a pick up of the wedding décor, and ending with a welcome party at my parents' house.

Friday—A day bombarded with tux fittings, checking into the NOVA Hotel, rehearsing the ceremony, and concluding with the rehearsal dinner!

Saturday—This would be the most crucial page in the timeline! Margot would live by the master schedule that covered everything from vendor drop-offs, bridal party schedule, photo timeline, and the event timeline.

Sunday—A day of rest, including the La Chapelle family brunch in the suburbs and the Trelenberg family brunch at the NOVA Hotel.

Monday—I'd be taking care of all of the boring stuff like vendor pick ups, organizing boxes of returned decorations, and writing thank-you notes.

Tuesday—The whirlwind of events would conclude with our private Catholic ceremony at St. Rita's. Hallelujah!

i do

BBQ SCHEDULE

12:00 PM	PUT WINE IN FRIDGE TO CHILL, ADD WATERS TO COOLER	MOM
1:00 PM	FLOWERS ARE DELIVERED CATHY FLOWERS	DAD
1:15 PM	SET UP TABLES & CHAIRS	PETER
1:30 PM	SET UP TABLES W/ MASON JAR ARRANGEMENTS, LINENS, ETC.	MOM
2:30 PM	SARA HEADS HOME TO SHOWER FOR PARTY	
3:15 PM	PUT OUT I DO BBQ SIGN IN FRONT OF THE HOUSE, PUT OUT PEACH CANDIES	DAD
4:00 PM	BBQ CATERING DROPPED OFF	MOM
4:00 PM	CHEESE BEING DELIVERED	MOM
4:30 PM	PREP SIGNATURE COCKTAIL & MASON JARS ON THE COFFEE BAR	BRO
5:00 PM	**PARTY STARTS**	
6:30 PM	SARA & PETER DIG UP WHISKEY	
8:00 PM	**PARTY ENDS**	
8:15 PM	GROOM ESCORTS GUEST OUT, TAKE FRIENDS TO THE WP	
8:30 PM	SPRAY TAN - SARA & MOM SHOWER	
8:35 PM	SARA & LAURA SPRAY TAN	
9:45 PM	PETER RETURN HOME	

As you can see, the wedding weekend was a spectacle. I was supervising four events, thirty-five vendors, thirteen bridesmaids, twelve groomsmen, one flower girl, one ring bearer, and four emotional, overbearing parents!

Wedding Schedule Advice

A wedding schedule will make even the most complex wedding weekend a breeze!

- **Start with a master timeline.** This should start on the first day of your wedding events and run through the last. Incorporate **every** little detail, including wakeup times, any pick-ups or drop-offs, and everything that needs to happen, even if it doesn't directly apply to you. Delegate every task that needs to be completed. It helps your crew know who needs to do what in case you can't be there or don't have time for questions.

- Make a specific timeline for *these* vendors weeks in advance:

  - **Hair and makeup**—You need everyone dressed and ready **on time!** Don't give a bridesmaid the earliest time if you know they sleep late! They will most likely miss their appointment.
  - **Photo and video**—Include a list of photos you want taken.

- Transportation—Guests can't use the provided transportation if you don't tell them when/where!
- Entertainment—Provide a detailed overview of when you want your emcee to announce key events (speeches, cake cutting, bouquet toss).

- **Review the vendor schedule.** Hiring a wedding planner does not mean the timeline is seamless! As I reviewed the master schedule, I noticed the ballroom wouldn't be ready until 3:00 p.m. on Saturday, but my photographer scheduled the ballroom photoshoot at 2:00 p.m.! I was able to catch this and arrange for the ballroom to be ready in time.

- **Make separate timelines for the bridesmaids, groomsmen, and parents!** Each party is responsible for different things. Create a timeline that is easy to follow to ensure everyone knows their role.

- **Give everyone a small role!** Family and friends want to help! Delegate tasks, big or small, to those you trust. If you give a bunch of small tasks to different people, there is a greater likelihood of them getting done because that is their only job. I gave each bridesmaid a task. Ansley would carry emergency feminine products, Amelia would stash snacks in her clutch, Samantha would bring Advil, Evan would sign the delivery for breakfast and lunch, and Vivienne and Kristen would be in charge of getting the bridal party to photos on time.

The Budget Bride

Don't be overwhelmed by the various wedding planning tools available on the internet. I used Google Sheets, a free app, to create my timeline. It was simple to use and easy to share with all parties involved.

THE DETAIL SHOOT

I scheduled a wedding detail photoshoot for the Thursday before the wedding. I can hear you asking, "But, Sara, what exactly is this?"

The photographer and videographer typically arrive early on the wedding day to style and capture the invitations and bride's accessories. The creative crew will style as many details as time permits, such as the vow books, rings, jewelry, and party favors. This is, surprisingly, one of the most time-consuming tasks for the photographer. It takes roughly thirty minutes just to style the wedding invitation and another fifteen minutes to photograph it.

Despite not knowing the benefits of getting these photos out of the way ahead of time, I scheduled a detail photoshoot the Thursday before the wedding.

My mom and I had an ongoing argument on where my bridesmaids and I would get ready the morning of the wedding. She wanted us to get ready at her house, and I wanted to get ready at the NOVA Hotel, a few minutes away from The Brantley Hotel. I was focused on convenience and proximity to the venue, while my mom was fixated on a daydream. She described a scene of my bridesmaids running around her professionally decorated house in blush silk robes, drinking coffee out of her Blue Willow China. The second I was engaged, she rambled on about how gorgeous her house would be for wedding photos, and how my bridesmaids and I **had** to get ready there.

As delightful as it sounded, I shut down the idea immediately. My parents live forty-five minutes (an hour in traffic) from the city, and the thought of one bride, thirteen bridesmaids, and one flower girl commuting to the ceremony in gowns sounded like a recipe for disaster.

I offered a compromise. "Mom, how about we take photos of all the wedding details at your house before the weekend begins?"

"What do you mean?" my mother asked.

"Well, your house is much prettier than a hotel room for photos. I can have the photographer and videographer come out before the wedding and take photos and an aerial tour of your house. It will **look** like we got ready at your house. Plus, it will be less stressful on the wedding day. I won't be waking up to cameras in my face." I sold her on the idea.

I arranged a shoot with my photo and video vendors and hired Margot as my creative director. A week before the photoshoot, I emailed the team a detailed shot list and schedule beginning at 10:00 a.m., with a firm stop at noon. In this two-hour window, we would capture my parents' house, my two wedding gowns, accessories, wedding rings, robes, the invitation suite, party favors, welcome bags, and other wedding trinkets.

On the Monday before the photoshoot, my mom called. "Hi, Sara, let Peter know that I hired Danielle to come over on Thursday morning to cut everyone's hair if he wants to get his hair cut."

"You did what?" I questioned in utter confusion.

"Danielle is coming over to cut my hair, CJ's hair, and Sam's hair around ten. Does Peter need his hair cut?" my mom asked.

I wasn't shocked by my mom's lack of awareness of the plans we had made. "Did you forget about the photoshoot we planned at your house that morning?" I asked, irritated with her utter disregard for the particulars. "We do not need to be running a hair salon in the background of my wedding photos. Are you out of your mind?"

"Sara, you're being selfish. We all need to get our hair cut." My mom hung up the phone.

I thought I was going to explode. I went out of my way to coordinate a photoshoot at the house for my mom. Between the detail photoshoot, transporting the wedding décor, and then setting up for the BBQ, I could **not** handle any last-minute wrenches thrown into my schedule.

I was able to reason with my mom and shift the salon party to my grandmother's house instead. If we stuck to the schedule on Thursday, the rest of the wedding weekend could go according to plan. But if we didn't complete our Thursday tasks, they would creep into Friday morning, which was already a busy day between the rehearsal and rehearsal dinner.

Before I knew it, it was the Thursday before my wedding, and I was a nervous wreck. I woke up minutes before my alarm and sprang out of bed at 6:30 a.m. to center myself with a twenty-minute yoga session. My mantra was, "be calm, be calm, be calm."

I headed to my parents' house thirty minutes before the photoshoot. I had all the items the photographer needed to shoot in labeled boxes for my wedding planner to take afterward. I did my best to stand back as the photographer and videographer peeled through my organized boxes to grab the accessories they wanted to style. In the corner of the room, I held my clipboard with my timeline and crossed off each shot as the team completed it.

The detail shoot ran smoothly, and I felt a thousand pounds lighter.

After the shot list was complete, our videographer privately recorded Peter's and my letters to each other. Typically, the morning of the wedding, the bride and groom exchange personal letters. Instead of reading the letter Peter wrote to me out loud, I recorded my letter to him. This was one of the better planning decisions. Reading my letter was emotional, and I'm grateful I didn't have to go there before the wedding.

Detail Shoot Advice

- **Do the detail shoot in advance if possible.** Prior to the day before the wedding, get as many tasks and errands done as possible! Having the detail photos complete before the wedding gave me a sense of relief.

- **Make a shot list beforehand:** Provide an outline of all of the shots you want your photographer to capture to make sure they don't miss anything.

- **You can photograph any meaningful wedding props.** This could include family heirlooms or wedding gifts your family gave you. Here is a list of items we photographed:

  - Invitation suite
  - Party favor
  - Rings
  - Vow books
  - Wedding day jewelry
  - Welcome gift
  - Wedding gowns
  - Wedding shoes
  - Wedding robes

For more photos, go to
www.thecovidbridebysara.com/post/details

THE PASS OFF

Immediately following the photoshoot, I returned the wedding details to their designated bins for Margot to transport to their destinations. Peter and I took ten trips each, running up and down my parents' stairs, carrying heavy plastic containers, and placing them by the door.

Margot joked, "I'm going to need a U-Haul to bring all of the décor to Atlanta."

Seeing the bins stacked by the front door, I realized this was no joke. Margot would need a U-Haul to transport everything to the venue because the car she drove to my parents' house might as well have been a golf cart. Accepting the challenge, Peter started a game of real-life Tetris to pack everything in the most efficient manner possible. I stood outside the car and cheered him on as he configured and finagled fifty percent of the decorations into the back, front, and sides of Margot's hatchback. There wasn't an inch of the car that wasn't put to use.

"Are you able to come back later for the rest of the stuff?" I asked, desperate to complete this task today.

"No, I have other obligations tonight," Margot apologized. "But I can be back here tomorrow at 8:00 a.m. for the rest."

Dang it! Now Peter and I have to hoist the rest of the bins back upstairs into the wedding workshop and out of plain sight for tonight's BBQ. Instead of complaining, I told her, "Great, thank you so much!" and sent Margot on her way.

I had an uneasy feeling about my items being split up.

I was unavailable the next morning to meet Margot, so my dad stepped in to help. It was really hard for me to delegate this task after the hours my mom and I slaved away in the wedding workshop. But in the end, I could only be in one place at a time, so I just had to roll with it.

Advice for Packing Your Wedding Details

- **Begin packing and organizing your boxes weeks before the wedding.** If you wait until the last minute to fetch your wedding details, you won't notice that items are missing or incorrect when there's still time to fix them. It is too late to reorder monogrammed napkins the day before the wedding if they are the wrong color.

- **Label a clear plastic bin with what is in the box, where it's going, and who is responsible for it.** This will limit confusion on what's in the boxes and where they need to go.

- To: Venue
- Location: Specific area at venue like Ballroom, Terrace, Cocktail Hour
- Items: List items in box
- Responsible Party: Person in charge of getting items there
- Contact Info: In case it is misplaced in transport

- **Pack all the boxes yourself and double-check to ensure everything is there!**

- **Make packing lists to help organize items.** Do this for yourself and the décor.

packing
LIST

BEAUTY
- ☐ BODY LOTION
- ☐ BLOW DRYER
- ☐ CHAPSTICK
- ☐ CURLING IRON
- ☐ CONTACTS/ GLASSES
- ☐ DEODORANT
- ☐ DRY SHAMPOO
- ☐ EYE CREAM
- ☐ EXTENSIONS/FAKE LASHES
- ☐ FACE LOTION
- ☐ FACEWASH
- ☐ HAIR BRUSH
- ☐ MAKEUP REMOVER
- ☐ PERFUME
- ☐ RETAINERS
- ☐ SHAMPOO & CONDITIONER
- ☐ TOOTHBRUSH & TOOTHPASTE

SLEEP, LOUNGE, UNDERGARMENTS
- ☐ BRIDAL PJS FOR SATURDAY
- ☐ BRIDAL ROBE & SLIPPERS
- ☐ BRIDESMAIDS ROBES & HANGERS
- ☐ PJS
- ☐ 2 SLEEP UNDIES
- ☐ 2 NUDE THONGS
- ☐ NUDE BRA
- ☐ NIPPLE PETALS
- ☐ STICKY BOOBS

OUTFITS
- ☐ REHEARSAL DINNER DRESS & SHOES
- ☐ SUNDAY BRUNCH DRESS & SHOES

BRIDAL ACCESSORIES & OTHER
- ☐ CASH FOR TIPS
- ☐ GARTER BELT
- ☐ HEADBAND
- ☐ LETTER & GIFT FOR GROOM
- ☐ VEIL
- ☐ WEDDING SHOES
- ☐ WEDDING HANDBAG
- ☐ WEDDING GOWN

EMERGENCY
- ☐ ADVIL
- ☐ BODY TAPE
- ☐ CASE OF WATER BOTTLES
- ☐ CHEESE ITS
- ☐ EYE DROPS
- ☐ KIND BARS
- ☐ LINT ROLLER
- ☐ STAIN REMOVER WIPES
- ☐ SEWING KIT
- ☐ SCISSORS
- ☐ TISSUES
- ☐ TIDE TO GO

THE I DO BBQ

My mother always underestimates the turnout and duration of a La Chapelle party. An insignificant gathering of ten turns into a full-blown soiree. My bridal shower that started at two o'clock in the afternoon ended up running until midnight on a Sunday! Because our parties always seem to get out of control, we were reluctant to host a welcome event at my parents' house, although it felt necessary to arrange some sort of event for family and friends traveling to celebrate Peter and me.

We couldn't expect everyone to sit in their hotel rooms alone and twiddle their thumbs all night. At first, my mom and I considered hosting a dinner at a nearby restaurant in Peachtree City but decided against it. The ideal scenario would be an open-house-style event where guests could swing by and say hi. Ultimately, we chose to host a gathering at my parents' house on the Thursday before the wedding. It would be a more welcoming and flexible environment than a restaurant.

My main concern with hosting at my parents' was my limited availability.

"I can handle everything," my mom promised again and again, but it wasn't long before the questions started coming: "How do I check the website for Thursday night RSVPs?" "Can you help me place a catering order?" "What decorations are we going to use?" "Where should I order the flowers from?"

I eventually took over planning because it was easier for me to directly manage rather than do so by proxy. Her questions piqued my interest, and I had a rush of energy in February after hosting a successful bridal shower; I was inspired to plan the welcome party. I revisited a lot of my ideas from the canceled engagement party, repurposing the Southern-vintage theme.

I went crazy ordering decorations to elevate the event from a mere gathering into a Georgia-peach-themed I Do BBQ. I ordered peach-colored napkins with "Sara & Peter" embossed in gold, peach tablecloths, a welcome sign with peaches on it, and even peach-colored candies to spread throughout the house in unique canisters (peach rings, peach saltwater taffy, peach slices).

Much like the scrapped engagement party plans, high-top tables would be placed around my parents' pool deck. Each table would feature an arrangement of white roses, white daisies, baby's breath, and greenery. I ordered extra florals to place around the house.

No party is complete without a signature cocktail; my brother Rob, who serves as the family bartender, created a recipe with juicy Georgia peach slices, gin, tonic water, fresh lime juice, and rosemary garnish from my parents' garden. The cocktail was so pretty that it deserved a glass of its own, so I hot-glued a lace burlap ribbon on fifty mason jars and purchased peach-colored straws to finish the look. We stocked the bar with wine, beer, and other spirits as well.

I ordered a stick-to-your-ribs kind of meal from the best barbecue joint in all of the South, Rock Sisters BBQ. We ordered pulled-pork sandwiches, barbecue chicken breasts, macaroni and cheese, spicy green beans, coleslaw, and brownies and cookies for dessert.

After going through the effort to hold the event, I only received thirty-five RSVPs, overwhelmingly from my family. I refreshed the RSVP link on my website a week beforehand, and the number was still the same. I was disappointed with the low turnout and another missed moment to shine and socialize during a well-planned event. However, I had a deep sense of relief that I didn't have to concern myself with hosting unfamiliar guests.

Two days before the I Do BBQ, Peter called me from work to tell me that a few of his friends and family members were going to stop by the BBQ. "Awesome, I can't wait! The party is going to be really nice. How many people do you think will come?" I asked.

"I think around fifteen people. Just a few of my family members and a couple of my groomsmen." Peter listed their names for me.

"Oh no, I only ordered enough food for thirty-five people! Let me call my mom." I hung up the phone in a panic and called my mom to share the news. "Hey, Mom, Peter said a couple of his family members and friends are going to make it tomorrow. Around fifteen more people. What should we do?"

"That's fine. Just call Rock Sisters BBQ and see if they can increase our order to fifty guests. Could you order a cheese plate, too?"

"I'll call them now. I can order a cheese plate, but it's going to be around three hundred dollars for fifty guests. Is that okay?" I asked.

"Yes, nothing is worse than not having enough food at a party," my mom stressed.

I made the adjustments to our catering order and found an available charcuterie company for a last-minute oversized serving platter. I felt content with the changes and figured we would have more than enough food and drink for fifty guests.

The morning of the I Do BBQ, I was preoccupied with my photographer and videographer styling the wedding details. By the time I finished my tasks and drove back to my apartment to change, it was 4:30 p.m. Vivienne, my maid of honor, was already at my parents' house helping my dad finish with the decorations. The event started at 5:00 p.m. but it wasn't until 6:00 p.m. that we had a full house. Peter's family, including his cousins and grandparents, came to the party. It wasn't my first time meeting them, but this time I wasn't playing defense at an away stadium; I was able to be the host—my specialty!

Once the party started to buzz (as well as the guests), Peter and I directed everyone to the backyard for the Southern tradition of digging up the bourbon. Burying a bottle of bourbon upside-down at your wedding venue one month beforehand is said to ward off bad weather on your wedding day; I am far too superstitious to skip proper acknowledgment of the rain god of Georgia. Since we couldn't bury bourbon on the grounds of The Brantley Hotel, we buried it in my parents' backyard. Peter shoveled up the red Georgia clay and dusted off the bottle, then poured everyone a shot.

Peter's friends and family from California loved the tradition. "It must have worked," one of them noted, "because the weather channel read thunderstorms until today!" The week leading up to the wedding had been full of flash floods and thunderstorms.

As the evening progressed, I noticed the party continued getting bigger. At 8:00 p.m., the time the barbecue was intended to end, more people showed up with their suitcases in hand. By 8:30 p.m., we had one hundred and fifteen guests scattered throughout the basement, kitchen, patio, and backyard, eating, drinking, and playing cornhole and pool.

With all of these unexpected guests, I began to fret that there wasn't enough food and drink for everyone, but somehow, we fed over a one hundred guests with an order for fifty. Are you familiar with John 6:5–13, from the Bible? It's the story of how Jesus performed a miracle and was able to feed five thousand hungry men and women with only two fish and five loaves of bread. The same thing happened at our barbecue. We even had leftovers, with the exception of the booze.

At 8:45 p.m., my friend Katie arrived. She does mobile spray tans, and I'd hired her to come to my parents' house to give my mom and me a spray before the wedding. We didn't think the party would still be carrying on after almost four hours.

I pulled my mom aside to tell her it was time to shower and get her spray tan, but she balked. "Are you out of your mind? I can't get a spray tan now!"

As impolite as it was for me to leave my own party, I quietly ran upstairs to prepare for my spray tan. While Katie was setting up her equipment in my childhood bedroom, I rushed into the shower. An even spray tan requires proper exfoliation and removing all traces of makeup. Think of it as preparing your canvas.

I could hear the hubbub of the party from upstairs, but I did what I had to do. Katie sprayed me down the exact number of times we agreed upon after months of trial sprays. I wanted to land on the right shade of I'm glowing, but I'm not orange. I waited for my spray tan to dry before slipping into my baggiest long sleeve t-shirt and unflattering sweatpants and bolted for the back door to avoid being caught in my heinous ensemble. I couldn't risk ruining my spray tan with a spilled drink or one too many hugs. On our way out, Katie and I were seen by a few, but did our best to remain incognito.

Eventually, Peter moved the party to Main Street, a strip lined with bars and restaurants. My parents' house was finally quiet, and by midnight, my parents had finished cleaning up. Peter didn't return to our apartment until one in the morning, after an evening of beers and shots with his friends. Long story short, our lame barbecue of thirty-five guests mushroomed into an event for the books. We never expected to host a raging party the night before our rehearsal dinner!

The next morning, the La Chapelle household was running short on sleep and long on coffee, and at our apartment, Peter did his best to butter me up. He felt guilty for keeping me waiting until the wee hours of the morning for him to come home. He felt even guiltier about being hungover.

I wasn't mad at Peter and felt happy he got the night of drinking out of his system. "Now promise me you had your fun, and you will go home early tonight," I insisted. "Looking good tomorrow is paramount!"

Welcome Party Advice

- **Stick to your predetermined schedule.** Leaving the welcome party to stick to my schedule wasn't easy, but I did what I had to do. Don't feel pressured to skip appointments in your pre-wedding routine just because a friend shows up at your door unexpectedly. My mom was upset that she never got her spray tan, but she didn't have a nearby apartment to escape to like I did.

- **Don't feel bad or apologize for doing what you need to do.** Each decision leading up to the wedding is either going to bolster a positive experience or strip away your plans. Ignore negative family members, turn down that third cocktail, and do not apologize for taking alone time. Do everything you can to prepare yourself mentally and physically for your wedding so you can be the best version of yourself that day.

THE
REHEARSAL DINNER

Two weeks before the rehearsal dinner, I was working double-time to replan the ceremony, collect RSVPs, send reminders for the new ceremony location, and throw together a grand exit. In the middle of the mayhem, I got a call from Mrs. Trelenberg.

"Hi Sara, I was wondering if I could ship some of the items I bought for the rehearsal dinner to your house?" she asked.

I was at a loss for words. I didn't know how to politely decline her request, but she was unaware of the level of commitment it would be for me to take ownership of tracking down her shipment and then organize it in my wedding workshop.

"I don't know if that's a good idea. I have an entire bedroom overflowing with stuff for the I Do BBQ, the wedding, and the Sunday brunch. I can't guarantee your items won't get lost in the shuffle." I was truly sorry I couldn't help.

Not recognizing my sincere apprehension, she continued. "It's only a few things. Just a welcome sign, napkins, a USC flag..."

"I'm worried they might get mixed up when my wedding planner comes to get everything on Thursday!" I tried to explain how this was a bad idea, especially since I had welcome signs, napkins, and other similar items.

"That's fine. Would you mind if I borrowed your microphone and amp for the rehearsal dinner speeches?" She remembered my professional mic and amp used at my bridal shower to play games.

"Yes! No problem!"

Volunteering Peter, she replied, "Great, I'll just have Peter bring them to the rehearsal dinner."

Ever since Peter started his new job in January, he'd been preoccupied and useless in the wedding planning arena. If it weren't for me, the man wouldn't have had a pair of clean socks or a home-cooked meal. If this became Peter's job, it would become my job. He would ask me to remind him to do it on the day of, meaning I would need to include it in my wedding schedule.

"Peter is really slammed with his new job, and I don't want to put anything else on his plate," I cautioned. "He hasn't even ordered his groomsmen a gift, and we're getting married in twelve days!"

Relentless, she replied, "That's okay, I'll have Peter do it! Thank you."

I was independently responsible for the success of the wedding, and I had been carrying the weight on my shoulders for months. Adding the lightest feather on top would break me, and saying I was overwhelmed was an understatement. I had put my career on the backburner for months, my mental health was on the fritz, and my social life was nonexistent.

I couldn't get the conversation with Peter's mom out of my head, so I called my dad to get some perspective. "I'm worried I'm making the worst impression, but I can't take responsibility for anything else."

My dad did his best to ease my mind, "Don't let it bother you! Just continue to be kind and take it off your list. If they remember to grab the mic and amp at the barbecue, then great. If not, it's no big deal. You have enough on your plate."

I scratched *pick up microphone and amp* off of my to-do list, but I couldn't forget that it needed to be done. For two days straight, I ignored my inclination to take responsibility for the microphone and amp until I finally surrendered and added it back to my wedding timeline.

I've heard jokes about the future in-laws like, "the best mother-in-law is one that lives very far away," or people referring to their mother-in-law as the monster-in-law, but I never figured I would be in a situation where my husband's family felt indifferent about me. I had no idea if Mrs. Trelenberg was warming up to the idea of me or not, so I was concerned about how the rehearsal dinner would end up.

I'm delighted to announce that I worried for no reason, and Mrs. Trelenberg hosted a thoughtful and elegant rehearsal dinner. For the event, she bought out one of the restaurants I recommended, Occe, a renowned European-inspired restaurant that serves a farm-to-table menu. My future mother-in-law decorated the contemporary and upscale space from top to bottom. There wasn't a detail I missed; she incorporated my **favorite everything**, colors, florals, signature cocktail, food, and even dessert.

At the entryway, she posted a picture of Peter and I sitting on top of the Lincoln Memorial. Waiters passed out Aperol Spritzes. The tables were set with a custom menu and centerpieces of peonies, carnations, freesia, and pink spring florals. As a party favor, she even bought macarons and placed a box at each seat. There were custom napkins, a professionally made pink balloon arch, and even a USC grooms' cake for Peter. She planned a lovely evening, and I was brimming with love and appreciation for her and her family.

Cocktail hour transitioned into dinner, and dinner led to speeches. There were six toasts and one roast from my bridesmaid Samantha. I laughed, and I cried, and I thanked the Trelenbergs for the wonderful event.

By 8:30 p.m., wedding guests began to trickle in for the open bar until 10:00 p.m. They gathered by the bar and listened to the speeches that ran late.

On the detailed timeline I provided to my bridesmaids, I made a note for Vivienne and Evan to escort me out of the rehearsal dinner and welcome drinks by 9:30 p.m., **no exceptions**. When the speeches ended at nine twenty-five, they made a direct line toward me to remind me of the time.

"Sara, it is almost nine-thirty!" Vivienne pointed at her watch.

Evan, my party friend, looked back at the bar. "Are you still wanting to go? A bunch of people are walking in and waiting at the bar to see you!"

I stood up from the table with a slice of groom's cake and hastily finished another bite. "Yes! I am ready to go!" I mumbled with a full mouth.

For the second night in a row, I had nursed my drinks and made the responsible decision of leaving early. I was really proud of myself for not drinking, especially when the signature cocktail was my favorite!

"Great! Let's go," Vivienne announced.

Evan and Vivienne escorted me to the door, only allowing me to stop to snag a photo like a celebrity leaving a red-carpet event. Out of the corner of my eye, I caught a glimpse of friends I hadn't seen in over a year because of COVID. It was unnatural for me to do so, but I fought the urge to greet them all. I felt rude, dodging eye contact from those who traveled from near and far to celebrate us, but I knew if I said hi to one person, I would get sucked into the black hole, making it impossible to leave.

I had to persuade myself it was more important to get a full night's sleep because tomorrow was going to be the biggest day of my life. Vivienne and I successfully made an Irish exit, leaving without saying goodbye. I caught my parents waiting in line for their car at the valet.

"Vivienne, I'll just ride with them. Thank you for getting me out of there on time!" I hugged her.

I hopped in my car with my parents, and they drove me six minutes down the road to the NOVA hotel. I felt like a child buckled in their backseat. It was the last time my parents would drop me off as a single woman. That car ride brought my emotions to a peak, and I told them how much I loved them and how thankful I was for their love and support. I stepped out of the car and headed to my bridal suite.

© *Willett Photo*

Rehearsal Dinner Advice

- **Be gracious.** Make sure to acknowledge your in-laws for hosting the rehearsal dinner (if they planned it, of course). The bride gets all the credit when it comes to the wedding, so throw the groom and his family a bone. Make the rehearsal as much about them as possible.

- **Switch up your look.** For the rehearsal dinner, I wore my hair in a high, sleek ponytail with a short, baby-doll-style dress. Try to wear a different hairstyle and outfit type. If you are wearing your hair up for your wedding, go with your hair down for the rehearsal. If your wedding gown is sophisticated, go with a playful and youthful look for the rehearsal.

- **Allow time for speeches.** During your wedding reception, you won't have time for more than a couple of speeches. The rehearsal dinner is an excellent time for close family and friends to say a few words.

- **Call it a night when it's time.** Stick to your guns and make a graceful exit when it's time. Enlist a friend or relative if you need help with this.

For more photos, go to
www.thecovidbridebysara.com/post/rehearsal

THE NIGHT BEFORE
THE WEDDING

My parents still tell the tale of their disastrous wedding eve, where my mom missed her bachelorette party, and my dad got so drunk, he almost missed their wedding the next day.

My mom planned to meet her girlfriends in Manhattan, only a forty-five-minute drive from her house in New Jersey. On her way to her bachelorette party, she stopped at the airport to pick up a bridesmaid traveling from New Orleans. While she drove toward the promise of her bachelorette party in New York City, her friend began smoking weed in the car. My mom had never been one to smoke marijuana or consume more than two alcoholic beverages, so it's no shock she ended up missing her exit and getting caught up in a two-hour detour in Pennsylvania. Let's just say her bridesmaid hotboxing her car was not the brightest idea.

It was midnight by the time my mom got to the end of the detour from hell, and she decided to just drive back to New Jersey and call it a night. When she got home, the front door was locked, and she had to wait on the front stoop until 3:00 a.m. for her sisters to return home with the key. Can you imagine missing your own bachelorette party to drive a four-hour round-trip to nowhere! This was the kind of incident that happened before the age of smartphones and GPS!

My dad, on the flip side, was celebrating his bachelor party in New Jersey at some local dive bar with his Sigma Chi buddies from college. They did a fine job dusting off the bottles from the top shelf to celebrate the last hoorah. His friend Big Al picked a fight with meathead locals, leading the twenty-one-year-old fraternity brothers to flee the bar. My dad's bachelor party ended prematurely, and he headed home at a reasonable hour.

Just as my dad turned the key to his hotel room, his uncle caught him in the hallway. "Bobbie L.A., let me take you out! No excuses!" his uncle coerced.

My dad turned and headed to another dive bar, despite declining the invitation twice. His uncle hazed him, making him match him drink for drink, and kept him out until two o'clock in the morning. The next day, my parents' church wedding ceremony started. My grandpa walked my mother down the aisle, but when she got to the top, my father was nowhere to be found. After what must have felt like an eternity, my dad finally dashed out of the chapel room and sprinted to the altar. He was so out of it, he didn't realize the ceremony had started. At the reception, he toasted with a glass of milk, nursing his hangover all day.

Both of my parents were exhausted on their wedding day and claim it was all a blur. I grew up hearing those stories and vowed to myself I'd not let something stupid happen before my wedding night.

The rehearsal dinner speeches ran an hour over schedule, but I stuck to my plan. Leaving early meant I missed out on the chance to greet my friends who had been waiting at the bar since 8:30 p.m. I was so committed to getting the sleep I needed that I didn't even risk saying goodnight to Peter. He was surrounded by friends from Los Angeles whom he's been begging me to meet for years. I couldn't risk walking over to kiss him goodnight without being introduced to six new faces. As hard as it was for me to leave, I knew I needed to go.

My parents dropped me off at the NOVA hotel and continued home to Peachtree City. I was staying at the same hotel as my guests but, luckily, avoided seeing anyone on my way to the penthouse suite.

When I got to my hotel room, I slipped off my Valentino Rockstud heels and wandered around the perimeter of the room. The one hundred and eighty-degree penthouse view of the sparkling city skyline took my breath away. Still feeling nostalgic from the car ride with my parents, I thought, *This will be the last night I will have as a single woman. This is my last view of the city skyline as a single woman.* I relished the moment and soaked in the view fit for a *Forbes* feature.

I was so enamored by the skyline and deep feelings of gratitude, I called my parents to thank them again. "Hey, guys. I just wanted to say thank you again. I am standing in the living room of my bridal suite overlooking the **entire** city of Atlanta. I wish you could see the view at night; this place is breathtaking."

"I'm glad you like it," my dad said. "Now get some rest."

"I feel so blessed; I love you guys." I hung up the phone and headed to the bathroom to begin my nighttime routine.

I slowly deconstructed my look, starting with my thick winged eyeliner, unraveling my sleek, high ponytail, and peeling off my dry contacts. I ended my beauty routine by adding a thick layer of moisturizer from head to toe until I resembled a glazed donut. Last, I took one melatonin sleep gummy and a small swig of NyQuil to help me fall asleep and stay asleep.

I was on the right track to getting the best night's sleep of my life. It was 10:15 p.m., and I was almost ready for bed. I pulled the blackout curtains shut, dropped the A/C down to sixty-eight degrees, and hopped into bed. I couldn't fall asleep without saying goodnight to Peter, so I tried to call him, but he didn't answer. I called him one more time before turning off my phone.

He answered. "Hi, what's up?" I could hear the noisy bar in the background.

"Oh, I'm so glad you picked up! I'm so sorry for leaving without saying goodbye. I just called to say goodnight."

"No worries, I knew you wanted to get to bed."

"Don't stay out too late! Tomorrow is the biggest day of our lives," I reminded.

"I won't! I promise. I love you."

"I don't need to remind you what happened the night before my parents' wedding, do I?" I asked with a laugh. "Love you, too! Sleep well." I hung up the phone and switched the settings to silent and do not disturb. I chugged a liter of water that was sitting on the nightstand, turned on my white noise sound machine, and slid my eye mask down. I took long and slow breaths to calm my nerves and put myself to sleep.

Instead of sleeping, I was up and down over the next two hours going to the bathroom. *What was I thinking, drinking water right before bed?* I checked my phone and saw it was already **midnight**! I knew I shouldn't have looked because it only made me more anxious about not sleeping. Fifteen minutes later, I went back into the bathroom for the third time and prayed to God I wouldn't have to go again until the morning. I laid back down in the cool, comfy king bed and closed my eyes. I **finally** fell asleep.

At 12:40 a.m., my phone started ringing.

The startling sound shook me to my core. My heart fell out of my chest, and my mind immediately went to the worst possible scenario. *Did Peter get cold feet? Did someone die! It can't be good. No one in their right mind would call **me** this late the night before my wedding.* With adrenaline pulsing through my veins and my heart beating out of my chest, I grabbed my phone to see who was calling.

It was my younger cousin Stevie. I immediately rejected the call.

I put my phone on do not disturb and airplane mode. How in the world did he get through? He must have called multiple times in a row, disabling my do not disturb feature for emergencies. I noticed that my phone was connected to the hotel internet, allowing Wi-Fi calling to go through. *I'll **never** make that mistake again.*

After the alarming phone call, my body and mind could not relax. I was wired and tense, so I grabbed a washcloth, ran it under cold water, and placed it over my eyes and forehead. I lay in bed trying to meditate, but nothing helped. I checked the time on my phone. It was 2:00 a.m. I stumbled out of bed to grab another five milligrams of melatonin and another swig of NyQuil.

I don't recommend overdosing on sleep aids because you will only feel like a train ran over you in the morning, but I was desperate for sleep.

I tossed and turned for another hour and checked my phone again. It was now 3:00 a.m., and I had only slept for thirty-five minutes. I calculated how many hours of sleep I could get if I fell asleep on the spot. I could still get five hours of sleep if I fell asleep immediately.

Whenever I have trouble sleeping at home, I put on a podcast with a monotone speaker and dry subject. The more boring the topic, the better it is at getting me to sleep. I searched for a health podcast on Spotify and clicked on the latest episode. I set a sleep timer for an hour and tried to close my eyes and listen. The podcast was *How to Strengthen Memory*; the expert explained how the brain processes memories and shared tools to help retain information and enhance memory.

Ironically, the first piece of advice to help your brain process experiences and convert them into longterm memories was sleep. Your brain needs **at least** seven hours of sleep a night.

Great. I'm not getting any sleep, so I won't be able to remember my wedding day.

The next piece of advice was to associate memories with smell. The speaker gave an example of how a certain perfume or the scent of a home-cooked meal can trigger a memory.

Really!? The one thing I didn't pack was my favorite perfume. I packed a free sample I got from a Nordstrom order. *I won't even have a perfume to connect the memory of my wedding to!*

The third piece of advice was to take a deep breath and say

out loud, "I will always remember this." The expert said that this trick should not be overused because it will stop working if employed too often. He advised only using this trick when something is really, really special.

I think my wedding day counts as one of those memories.

The last piece of advice was to take photos and videos. Looking at photos and videos can trigger memories and help preserve moments.

Phew, at least that's taken care of. I have an awesome photographer and videographer.

The podcast shut off after an hour, and I was still awake. Usually, I fall asleep after ten minutes of listening to a podcast, but not this time.

It was now 4:00 a.m., and I was wide awake.

I watched my clock and finally had a shallow sleep from about 5:45 to 8:30 a.m. when my alarm went off. I'd slept a whopping two hours and forty-five minutes and was running on fumes.

Night before the Wedding Advice

Know that you'll make it through, but prep nonetheless! I've always struggled with sleep anxiety, but the night before my wedding was particularly unpleasant. However, I was able to get through my wedding, primarily because I followed my own advice below:

- **Do not drink too much!** I was not hungover for my wedding or the rehearsal dinner! I nursed my drink at the rehearsal dinner and the night before at the I Do BBQ. At the rehearsal dinner, I asked my waitress to keep bringing me virgin cocktails after my first drink. No one had any idea I was sipping club soda and lime.

- **Make sleep a priority the week before the wedding.** I made sure I turned off the TV by 9:30 p.m. and was asleep by 10:30 p.m.

- **Make sure you get enough sleep the night before the wedding!** If you are worried about getting a good night's sleep before the wedding, try these tips:

  - Assign a friend to hold you accountable for leaving the rehearsal dinner at a reasonable hour.
  - Wherever you are sleeping the night before the wedding, make it as comfortable and homey as possible. Pack whatever you need; if you need your pillow and blanket from home, bring it!
  - Turn off your cell phone and put it out of reach! I'm not sure if I would trust just an alarm clock or wake-up call, so assign someone to check on you to make sure you're awake.

THE MORNING OF THE BIG DAY

I usually don't need an alarm to wake me, but with a terrible night's sleep, the morning of my wedding was an exception.

My phone had thirteen missed calls, eleven text messages, and one voicemail. The first round of hair and makeup appointments started at 8:30 a.m., just as I was getting up, so my bridesmaids were already up and at 'em. Before returning any calls, I stumbled into the bathroom. I hardly had enough time to wash and dry my hair. My reflection was horrifying; my eyes were bloodshot and framed with dark, puffy circles, my skin was dull, and my lips were chapped. Overall, my body felt cold and sluggish. I'd had a better night's sleep on a discount flight to Spain, sitting in a nonreclining middle seat next to the bathroom, than I did in a plush king bed the night before my wedding. Regardless, it was game time, and I couldn't let my lack of sleep ruin the most important day of my life.

When I got out of the shower, my phone was ringing again. It was my mother. I spoke for the first time that morning, and I was caught off guard by my low, raspy voice. "Hey, what's up?" "Sara, did you take my strapless bra?" My mom implied I stole it. "I can't find it anywhere!"

"Mom, I did not take your bra. I promise."

"Well, you borrowed it last, and I need it. How can Dad get into your apartment to look for it?" she continued as though I'd said nothing.

This was such a classic Mom move. She was supposed to be at the hotel to start getting ready in an hour, and she couldn't find her bra. "Mom, first of all, your bra would **not** be at my apartment. Next, why are you just now trying to figure out what undergarments you are wearing? I've had my bra packed for weeks now!" I shouted back.

Upset and frazzled, she said, "Well, I can't find it, and you were the last person to wear it. I don't know what I'm going to do."

In the background, I could hear my dad suggesting that they run to the mall at 10:00 a.m. when it opened to buy a new bra. This was a much better idea than raiding my apartment for a nonexistent bra. It was only just 9:00 a.m., and my wedding day timeline already felt off.

"Oh shoot, it's nine!" I said out loud. "Gotta go. Bye!"

I'd ordered a catered breakfast for the bridesmaids that would be delivered to my suite in just moments. Sure enough, I heard a knock on the door. With no regard to my post-shower towel apparel and wet hair, I flung the door open to find my friend Evan.

"Oh, thank heavens!" I signaled her to come in. Evan helped arrange the catered breakfast and lunch, and she was there to accept and sign the first delivery. She was thrown off by my appearance because I'm usually ahead of schedule, **not behind.** Evan manned the door, set up the catering, and greeted my bridesmaids as they arrived while I frantically dried my hair.

Before joining the ladies, I changed into my getting-ready ensemble—a white matching PJ set made with satin and lace, white furry slippers labeled "Bride," and a sequined white robe with WEDDING DAY VIBES across the back.

"Ahh, it's your wedding day! How do you feel?" the girls screamed.

In a very honest and tired voice, I said, "I was so anxious last night I couldn't sleep a wink! I feel alright this morning. Just hoping I have energy for the day."

"Our bridal party is a mini-pharmacy," Vivienne pointed out. "I have Valium if you need it."

"Yes, I packed my vape pen," Samantha said. "That would have put you **right** to sleep."

Amelia added, "Sara, I packed prescription-strength sleeping pills. I could have given you one!"

If only I'd known those details last night! The bridal suite was full of energy, and I was having a tough time matching my friends' enthusiasm. I would respond with, "I feel fine! I'm fine. Today is going to be fine."

Samantha called me out, "We didn't ask how you were feeling, but clearly, you're doing fine!" She was right. I was delirious and couldn't engage in witty banter; I could only continue to convince myself that **I was fine.**

Before heading down to my hair and makeup appointment, I pulled an envelope from my suitcase addressed to Sara Belles. Peter and I spent hours handwriting letters to give to one another to read the morning before the wedding. I perched on the couch in the living room with the girls and began reading. I did my best to stay focused, but I was distracted by the background conversation and nerves. By the time I'd struggled through a quarter of the letter, it was 10:30 a.m., and I needed to grab my things and head to my hair and makeup appointment. Ten floors down, a four-person hair and makeup team was busy transforming my thirteen friends into red-carpet-ready bridesmaids.

Wedding Day Getting Ready Advice

- **Dedicate space for getting ready.** I highly suggest booking **two** hotel rooms: one for hair and makeup, and another for bridesmaids to get dressed, eat, and lounge before the wedding. You don't want to crowd your hair and makeup artists, and you definitely don't want to risk getting makeup on any of the gowns (especially yours)!

- **Feed your bridesmaids!** Provide breakfast and lunch for your bridesmaids. The morning is busy, and they won't be able to leave and find food on their own! Stock the getting ready room beforehand with extra snacks and water.

- **Delegate tasks to your bridesmaids.** On the morning of my wedding, I had spread the responsibilities amongst the girls, whether that be signing for the food delivery or reminding others to get to their hair and makeup appointments. With so much going on, it's best to make each bridesmaid feel accountable for a small part of the day.

- **Don't check your phone the morning of the wedding.** You will only be bombarded with text messages of congratulations, family and friends asking where they need to be and when, and last-minute wedding guest dropouts. Even with the small hiccups, I managed to remain calm the entire morning.

- **Be in the moment.** Don't worry about Instagram or posting real-time updates of your wedding. None of that matters. The people you are supposed to spend time with are going to be within arm's reach.

The Budget Bride

Host the getting-ready party at your apartment, house, or nearby friend's house to avoid paying for hotel rooms. If you can, stock the getting-ready area with a case of water, granola bars, bagels, oatmeal, apples, bananas, and other simple and mess-free foods that are cheaper than catering.

For more photos, go to
www.thecovidbridebysara.com/post/morning

THE HAIR
AND MAKEUP
APPOINTMENT

Nine months before the wedding, I booked my hair and makeup vendor. I met Liz five years ago when I competed in the Miss Georgia pageant. I had taken her hair and makeup class, and she taught me about cosmetic products, the proper tools, and the latest techniques. Liz is the only artist I trusted; the wrong artist can make my face look weathered and masculine. I have big hazel eyes, bushy eyebrows, a prominent nose, and a strong jawline, features that can be problematic for some artists. Even with our past history, it still took us **two** hair and makeup trials to reach a result we were happy with.

I made a point to hire enough artists to attend to my large bridal party. Brides rarely book enough hair and makeup artists to complete their bridesmaids in a timely manner, so the first appointments often begin around 7:00 a.m., which is brutal. I always happen to have the first appointment, so

I'm speaking from experience. I wanted my bridesmaids to sleep in the morning of my wedding so they felt energized and refreshed.

I did everything I could to hire Liz's extended team of six artists, but COVID restrictions made that impossible. Policy required artists to have a six-foot distance between beauty stations, and the hotel suite barely had the space to configure four stations. This forced my morning timeline to begin at 8:30 a.m. instead of my ideal start time of 10:00 a.m. I could have captured another hour and a half of sleep if not for the virus that had already disrupted so much of my wedding landscape!

When I hired Liz, I asked Mrs. Trelenberg who from her family would need services. She responded with just her and her mother. I proceeded with booking appointments and scheduling the timeline. Two months leading up to the wedding, I paid the final invoice and set aside cash for tips and parking.

Two weeks before the wedding, Mrs. Trelenberg asked if Liz could add two more appointments to the morning schedule. I knew it wouldn't be possible with the limited number of artists and tight schedule. Instead of shooting down her request, I said, "Let me check with Liz. I don't think she has the bandwidth for additional appointments. If that's the case, I'm happy to share the contacts of some other makeup artists in Atlanta who will do a great job."

After speaking with Liz, she confirmed that she hardly had enough time to complete the sixteen appointments already scheduled. In order to include two more, she would have to shift her start time to 7:15 a.m. for my bridesmaids. I felt at fault relaying this information to Mrs. Trelenberg because I really didn't want to appear difficult and unaccommodating.

Mrs. Trelenberg decided to keep her appointment with Liz's team and booked another team for her family members. The morning of the wedding, she ended up canceling her appointment with Liz. After feeling responsible for not being able to meet Mrs. Trelenberg's request, she backed out of the appointment anyway. Per usual, I think too much about the smallest things and realized I shouldn't have stressed over the appointments in the first place.

When it was time, I headed down to the other bridal suite for my beauty appointment. I could hear music playing from down the hallway, only amplifying how tired I felt when my energy was out of sync. When I opened the hair and makeup suite door, I got a breath full of hairspray. Four of my bridesmaids were sitting in directors' chairs getting dolled up. Minutes later, my mom arrived with my dad.

"You made it!" I applauded.

"It's good luck," my dad said as he came into the room.

"What is?" I questioned.

"Mom losing her bra! She lost her bra the morning of **our** wedding, and we've been married for thirty-seven years!" He took a look around the hotel suite packed with floor-length mirrors, ring lights, hair tools, and a table of cosmetics. "I better get out of the war zone. I'll see you at one-thirty."

My dad was right! For as long as I could remember, my mom has complained about how she lost her padded bra on her wedding day. She claims that one of her bridesmaids stole it, but on further reflection, she probably just misplaced it. Thirty-seven years later, on the morning of **my** wedding, she lost her bra again. It must be an omen for a long, happy marriage.

My mom and I settled in our chairs to begin our hair and makeup transformations. Instead of a peaceful experience getting ready, my mom was screaming into her phone, directing my cousins on where to be for the wedding and at what time. She finally hung up the phone when my florist came in to deliver my bridal bouquet. I gushed over the lush spring bouquet made from blush and white peonies, garden roses, and ranunculus, with the teeniest hint of greenery. The semistructured bouquet was wrapped in a whimsical white and blush velvet ribbon that draped down effortlessly.

I thought it was impeccable...until my florist left the room.

"Wasn't your bouquet supposed to be all white?" my mom asked in confusion. "Didn't we ask for an all-white bouquet?"

She was right. We'd decided on an all-white bouquet, but there was nothing we could do about it now. "It's going to be fine. It's beautiful. Can we please not talk about anything that goes wrong today?" I begged her.

Moments later, there was another knock on the door. It was my future mother-in-law. Mrs. Trelenberg entered the room with her hair set in an elegant French twist. "I am just about to kill my family! I paid for four hair and makeup appointments, and everyone is too hungover to make it. I took one of the appointments this morning, so the stylists at least got to do something," Mrs. Trelenberg said. Her low and raspy voice highlighted how late the last two nights had been for her.

"It's been such a hectic morning," I shared.

We chatted while Liz finished my hair and makeup. Simultaneously, my bridesmaids were getting the party started in the suite above us, popping bottles of champagne. Once I was finished, I headed back upstairs to check on everyone.

© *Willett Photo*

Wedding Hair and Makeup Advice

- **Schedule a hair and makeup trial before the wedding.** This is essential to do! Don't expect the artist to get it right for the first time on your wedding day. It took me two trials, and we still made adjustments the day of. If you will have a spray tan on your wedding day, get a spray tan before your trial. You want your artist to be able to write down the colors, shades, and products used in the practice runs to make your wedding day go smoothly! Last, bring all of your accessories with you to the trial. The first hairstyle I tried overpowered the diamond hoops I wanted to wear for the wedding, so I ended up switching my hairstyle.

- **Bring photos to your trial appointment.** Having a photo of a hairstyle or makeup you like will help your stylist, big time! It's a lot easier to show a picture of what you like than it is to describe what you want! After your trial, take photos to see how you look in pictures. Have the photos handy on the wedding day to jog your stylist's memory.

- **Be honest with how you feel in your hair and makeup!** First and foremost, don't be afraid to tell your stylist that you **don't** love the final product. He or she is there to make sure you love how you look on your wedding day. In my case, we tested a hairstyle that required clip-in extensions, and I was head over heels with the way it looked. But, in being truthful with myself, I told Liz that the extensions felt heavy and made my head hurt. We switched my hairstyle to a look that was light enough to wear all day.

- **Make sure you look like yourself.** If you don't usually wear a bold red lipstick, why would you wear it for your wedding day? Don't catch your husband by surprise by looking like an entirely different person on your wedding day. You want to look like a **better** version of yourself on your wedding day—not someone else!

- **Pick a color palette and hairstyles for your bridesmaids!** Don't let your bridesmaids go rogue on hair and makeup! Select one to three hairstyles for the girls to choose from, keeping in mind what is feasible with their natural hair lengths. Also, choose an eyeshadow and lipstick that complement their dresses. You want everyone's colors to look similar. You don't want one bridesmaid with a hot pink lip and the other in a red, and another in a brown pink. For example, I chose Mac Whirl Lip Liner and Nymphette Mac gloss—many of the girls purchased the lip color beforehand so they could reapply throughout the wedding day.

- **Don't require your bridesmaids to pay for professional hair and makeup.** Give them the option. If someone can't afford the services, and you want everyone to look the same, pay for it yourself.

- **Don't start the appointments too early!** If the first round of appointments begins at 7:00 a.m., and photos aren't until 3:00 p.m., those early appointments will need touch-ups.

- **Set a schedule for wedding day appointments.** Don't ask your bridesmaids to be on standby. Give them a designated time to be ready to go with clean, dry hair.

  - 8:15 a.m.: Mollie, Hannah, Kathy
  - 9:15 a.m.: Maid of Honor, Matron of Honor
  - 10:15 a.m.: Bride, Mother of Bride, Mother-in-Law

THE TIME TO
GET DRESSED

My mom and I finished our beauty appointments and headed upstairs to the penthouse to get dressed. When we arrived, the girls were drinking champagne, blasting explicit rap music, and dancing around in their silk blush robes that were significantly skimpier in person than online. My baby cousins, the flower girl and junior bridesmaid, quietly sat in the corner of the room, mortified by their behavior.

My photographer arrived and lined up the bridesmaids and me for photos in our robes and then demanded that my mother and I change into our gowns **right away.**

Looking at a tray of untouched sandwiches, my mom said, "I'm starving, I need to eat something first."

"We need to change now!" I told her.

I must have alarmed my bridesmaids because all thirteen of them began frantically changing into their gowns. I tried to tell them they had an extra thirty minutes to change while

I was taking first look photos with Peter, but they couldn't hear me over the deafening music.

My mom and I were competing for space to change in the bedroom. Bras, robes, and heels were flying. In the bathroom, my mom was doing her best to wriggle into a fresh pair of Spanx, but every thirty seconds or so, another bridesmaid would bust into the bathroom and humiliate her in the middle of performing the Spanx hop. Since the bathroom wasn't any more private than the bedroom, she moved to sit on a bench at the foot of the bed to finish getting dressed.

Thump!

I heard a loud crash from the bedroom and sprinted into the room wearing only my thong and nipple pasties to see what had happened. My sixty-year-old, arthritis-ridden mother was on the floor! It's a rare occasion to see my mom on the floor, because she can't get back up on her own.

"Mom! Are you okay?" I cried. "What happened? Let me help you up." A fall could lead to broken bones or worse, and I was suddenly concerned we'd be taking an emergency trip to the hospital instead of pictures.

"The bench tipped over," my mom wailed from the floor. "There were girls on the other end, and when they got up, it tipped over!"

Vivienne and I helped her up.

Brushing off the incident, my mom said, "I feel fine. At least I landed on my butt." In that moment, she felt okay, and she didn't anticipate her fall leaving a lasting impact. Only later would we understand the toll it had taken.

We headed into the living room to finish securing my gown. It took four bridesmaids to figure out how to clip on my overskirt. Once it was fastened, it was time to go.

"I'm starving!" my mom said. "I still haven't gotten to eat anything. I am going to pass out if I skip a meal." Dressed in her evening gown, my mom grabbed a sandwich and took a few bites, cautious not to drop crumbs on the periwinkle beaded dress.

Just then, my dad knocked on the door to remind us that it was time to go for our first look. When my dad saw me for the first time, dressed in my wedding gown, my emotions burst like a helium balloon. The two of us walked toward each other; I could see my childhood flashing before his eyes as he stared back at me. My heart was overflowing with joy, nostalgia, anticipation, and butterflies. Today was the day his one and only little peanut was getting married.

With our eyes glossy with tears, my dad and I interrupted our special moment and, in unison, shouted, "Nope! We are **not** going to cry!" We laughed at our response, and I bent forward to dump my tears onto the floor to avoid mascara streaks down my cheeks.

While my dad and I were sharing this moment, the photographer captured my mom emotionless, shoveling a sandwich into her mouth. She didn't shed a single tear that day, but she was instrumental in keeping my dad and me from having an emotional breakdown. The Hallmark moment was interrupted when bright yellow mustard hit her gown.

© *Willett Photo*

THE FIRST LOOK

The first look is the moment when the couple sees each other for the first time on their wedding day. Deciding whether or not we would have a private first look before the ceremony was a controversial topic in the La Chapelle-Trelenberg household during the early stages of wedding planning.

When we hired our photographers, Bri and Barrett Thompson (known as Thompson Photo), we were asked whether or not we wanted a first look. We needed to make a decision early in the planning process because the rest of the wedding timeline would depend on it. This was when I discovered Peter's strong opposing stance on a first look before the ceremony. Peter believed it would lessen the experience of seeing me walk down the aisle for the first time. I couldn't argue his feelings on the matter, so I did my research and called my photographer.

"What are your thoughts on having a first look?" I asked Bri. "Peter doesn't want one."

"If your ceremony starts at 5:00 p.m., you would only have about forty-five minutes to capture pictures, and we won't have time to change location."

Before deciding, I wanted to meticulously assess our two options the best way I knew how—a pros and cons list.

Pros: (Have a first look)

- I'd enjoy the ceremony more if I wasn't worried about finishing to take photos.

- The natural light in the afternoon is much better for photos.

- Our wedding party would be free after the ceremony and could enjoy cocktail hour.

- The first look could be in a different location than the ceremony for more interesting photos.

- We could focus on just family photos after the ceremony.

- I'd be less anxious about walking down the aisle because I'd already know Peter's reaction.

- I would be less likely to cry at the ceremony.

Cons: (No first look)

- I wouldn't have a video of Peter crying as he catches the first glimpse of me walking down the aisle.

Seven pros to one con called for me to make an executive decision and plan a first look with Bri and Barrett. In time, I was able to convince Peter it was the right choice for us. They planned our first look in a park I'd never heard of, Lynn Park, with a lush European-inspired garden. Nestled in the middle of a quiet in-town neighborhood, it was less likely to have photobombers like bikers and runners. Our photographers would drive us separately; I would ride with Bri to the park, and Peter would ride with Barrett.

At 1:45 p.m. on the wedding day, Bri escorted me out of my bridal suite to head to our first look. She called her husband, Barrett, to make sure Peter wasn't lurking in the hallway or in view as I made my escape toward her car.

I did my best to stuff my oversized train into the backseat of her dusty Four Runner without getting any dirt on my diamond white gown. I took up the **entire** backseat of her car. The drive to Lynn Park felt surreal, and I sat quietly in the back seat, collecting my thoughts. I didn't know how I would react when I saw Peter for the first time in his wedding tux.

Barrett called to let Bri and I know that Peter was ready. Bri escorted me out of the car, and I took baby steps holding my train in my hands. I could see Peter's shiny blonde hair reflecting the sunlight. He stood tall and confidently, with his back to me.

When I got close enough to Peter, Barrett told Peter to turn around. This was the moment I expected myself to break into tears, but I was unbelievably calm. After my sleepless night and crazy morning, I felt a deep sense of peace. We locked eyes and relished in our (mostly) private moment. We still had two photographers, a videographer, and two assistants nearby.

Peter was dressed in a tailored white tux dinner jacket with a black lining. His bow tie was black with tiny white polka dots. His long hair was combed back like a charming Disney prince. I expected to shed a tear, but I felt more at home with Peter than I had that entire day. Peter has that effect on me; he makes me calm.

Other than the fact we got spectacular photographs in the soft spring afternoon light, the first look was not what I expected it to be. There was an awkward moment when I saw Peter for the first time. I had no idea what to say to him.

"You look so handsome."

"We're getting married today!"

"I didn't sleep at all last night."

"Have you had anything to drink today?"

"How has your day gone so far?"

I'm not sure what I expected the first look to be like. It's not like we came prepared to recite Shakespearean love sonnets to one another. Shortly after the first look, our parents arrived in a Mercedes Sprinter Van to take photos. Our bridal party of twenty-five friends followed shortly after in the white, old-fashioned trolley I rented for them. Shockingly, the rest of the afternoon went as planned.

The first look was a tad anticlimactic, but it was just what Peter and I needed. Even Peter agreed we made the right choice. We were able to see each other before our two hundred and fifty guests arrived.

© Willett Photo

First Look Advice

Determine whether or not you'll have a first look before the ceremony. Consider these factors:

- **What time is your ceremony?** If you have a 2:00 p.m. ceremony and a 5:00 p.m. reception, don't do a first look. There is plenty of time to take pictures after the ceremony. If you have an evening ceremony and reception, I highly encourage a first look.

- **Are you emotional?** If you don't want to cry during your ceremony, consider a first look to get those butterflies and that anxiety out of the way.

- **How photogenic are you?** I know we needed two opportunities to take photos together. Having a first look gave us the chance to get comfortable in front of the camera that day.

- **How big is your wedding party?** The bigger the wedding party, the more you should consider a first look. It is time-consuming to capture photos with a large bridal party.

For more photos, go to
www.thecovidbridebysara.com/post/firstlook

THE CEREMONY

Peter and I had a thirteen-month engagement but ended up only having three weeks to plan our wedding ceremony itself. After changing our ceremony to The Brantley Hotel, I was slightly relieved to be able to host the ceremony and reception in one location. There was less room for error, and frankly, I'd been through more than enough errors leading up to the big day. The day I canceled the church was the same day I met Margot at the hotel to scope out the space.

I would host the ceremony on the fifth-floor terrace, which was not the rooftop—though it is outside. It's located above the ballroom and was just high enough up from the street that it was somewhat insulated from the noisy traffic, but it wasn't tall enough to catch unobstructed views of the city skyline. Massive skyscrapers shade half of the terrace, making the space feel smaller than it actually is. The left side is open air, and the right side has a metal patio covering.

When Margot and I viewed the space, the rooftop was clear of furniture. It was vast, overwhelmingly concrete, and set in an urban and gray atmosphere. Looking at the situation with a glass-half-full mentality, I framed the terrace as a blank canvas, just waiting to be painted. It was going to take a small miracle to brighten the terrace and soften its urban edges.

Unlike the magnificent church, I was going to need to rent additional items to turn this concrete platform into a ceremony space. I began by making a list:

1. Seating for guests

2. Stage for ceremony

3. Microphones and speakers for the reverend, performers, readers, and us

4. An aisle runner

5. Lighting

6. Florals

I had no idea how I would afford all of these essential items with a growing deficit in my wedding bank account. I came to terms with accepting a higher-than-normal credit card balance.

Margot and I walked around the terrace multiple times before landing on the area to conduct the ceremony. We didn't want to orient the ceremony in the back left corner of the terrace, overlooking an eyesore of a parking lot. Unfortunately, there was no other way to situate two hundred and fifty guests.

Since the seating was flat, we needed a stage for Peter and me to stand on, making it possible for guests in the back to see. Behind the stage, I needed to come up with a design that would conceal the parking lot. A typical flower arch would not be enough. I imagined three rectangular structures with flowers draping across them.

Stretching from either end of the open-air patio, café lights would be strung to add a warm glow. Underneath the covered space, I imagined small fairy twinkle lights to add a touch of magic. Down the aisle, I was set on finding a turf runner; the rooftop was too gray, and the turf would add a pop of green for a garden feel. On either side of the aisle, I wanted low floral arrangements to pop with blush and white flowers.

For the ceremony seating, I pictured clear ghost chairs, which I typically don't like, but I needed the chairs to remain neutral to avoid overpowering the florals. I shared my million-dollar idea with my florist, who suggested mixing in white steel lanterns to make the overall price more reasonable without compromising the design. In my mind, I designed a European garden-style ceremony. Please don't Google European garden-style weddings and assume my ceremony was up to par. I could only do so much with my dwindling funds and time.

I worked day-in and day-out to bring our ceremony up from the ashes. If I couldn't rent the items I needed, I bought them. If I couldn't buy them, I made them. For instance, our venue did not have enough microphones or microphone stands, so I bought microphone stands and brought microphones I already owned to the ceremony.

We couldn't rent a stage that fit the rooftop dimensions, so Margot found a guy named Karl to build one for us. Yes, Karl **built** a custom stage. I am now the proud owner of a white, wooden stage. Give me a call if you ever find yourself in need of one.

I'm not going to lie and tell you that I handled these three weeks before the wedding with grace. I was stressed. I was angry. I was resentful.

Wedding planning went from a fun side hobby to a full-time job of designing, reviewing contracts, budgeting, and tracking invoices. People kept telling me to appreciate this time, and I thought they were crazy. It dawned on me why wedding vendors collect a fifty percent down payment up front. If they didn't request some form of prepayment, no one would ever have a wedding! There were times I was ready to pull the plug on the entire operation, but the only thing holding me back was the deposits I'd already paid.

The cherry on top of the last-minute ceremony change was having to text, email, or call our entire guest list. My mom, my dad, Peter, and I spent the Saturday before the wedding texting our guests to remind them. It was the first time the majority of the guests had received this piece of information.

Embarrassingly enough, text chains with my friends were constant reminders and updates for the wedding:

Sara: *Please RSVP on the website, my ex-wedding planner is holding my RSVP cards hostage.*

Sara: *Our reception is now taking place at The Brantley Hotel and NOT Braxton Country Club.*

Sara: *Our ceremony is now taking place at The Brantley Hotel. DO NOT go to church!*

If this book makes you want to elope, I don't blame you. You may be wondering if all of the stress and planning was worth it. I'm here to tell you that in the end, it was totally worth it.

My wedding ceremony was perfect, in every sense of the word.

After our photoshoot in the park, I returned to The Brantley Hotel and was escorted to a bridal suite with my dad, matron, and maid of honor, while the rest of the wedding party was directed to the ballroom to line up for the ceremony.

I had thirty minutes to regroup before walking down the aisle. When I got to the suite, my hair and makeup artist, Liz, was waiting with her bag of cosmetics and bobby pins. It had been four hours since my makeup was applied, and I needed a fresh coat of lip gloss and powder. I hadn't worn my veil for the first look, so it would still be a surprise for Peter, and that had to be pinned as well.

I slipped out of my heavy gown and threw on a robe while Liz performed her magic. My maid and matron of honor, Vivienne and Kristen, watched YouTube videos on how to tie our wedding bands onto the ring bearer's pillow. My dad stood at the window and watched the terrace filling from a bird's-eye view. I fought my urge to peek because I wanted to see my vision come to life for the first time when I floated down the aisle.

"Grandma and Grandpa are sitting on the wrong side of the aisle," he announced from his vantage point. "There won't be enough seats for family!" My dad began to fret.

When planning the ceremony, I reserved the exact number of seats needed for the families.

"Does someone have Margot's number? We need to fix this."

I flipped my dad a text with Margot's contact.

"Margot, I noticed that some of the families are sitting on the wrong sides," he told her. "Can you please fix this?" Relief washed over his face as he watched the families play musical chairs.

Liz finished my touch-ups, the girls secured the rings on the satin pillow, and my dad saved the ceremony. We still had twenty minutes to wait, so we raided the minibar for overpriced snacks.

"Does anyone have perfume?" I asked through a mouth full of trail mix. "I got the nervous sweats before our first look."

Kristen pulled out an expensive-looking bottle, "I have some right here!" she offered.

"You're the best!" I praised, taking the bottle. "I forgot perfume. And last night, I listened to a podcast on how smell can trigger memory. Now every time I smell your perfume, I will remember my wedding day!"

"No need, I already bought you a bottle," Kristen confided.

Ten minutes before the ceremony, I began to put on my wedding gown—I needed at least five minutes to clip on the overskirt. The second Vivienne and Kristen finished securing the gown, I had a confession to make. "I have to pee." I sounded guilty of a crime.

"That's okay, we have time. Let us help you in the bathroom," Kristen said.

"No, it's fine," I insisted. "It's probably just nerves." Vivienne and Kristen didn't take my response for face value, so they grabbed my fifteen-foot train and held it over my head while I used the restroom.

We now had three minutes until the ceremony, so I asked the girls and my dad to pray with me. In unison, we bowed our heads. "Dear Lord," I murmured. "Thank you for this beautiful day. I could not have gotten here without your faith. Pray for us as we embark on this journey together. Give us the energy, the strength, and the vitality we need to fully appreciate and relish in the love. Grant us peace and a sense of calmness. Speak through me when I say my vows, and dance through me during our first dance. Lord, let us feel your presence. Thank you for the blessings you continue to grant us, and may we never take you for granted. Amen."

I pulled out the second memory trick I had learned from the podcast the night before. I grabbed their hands and looked my dad, Vivienne, and Kristen in the eyes, and said, "I will always remember this moment. I love you all so much, and I will always remember this feeling." The trick was effective because I remember that moment vividly; my dad was on my right, Kristen in the middle, and Vivienne on my left. I remember the way they looked at me. I remember my dad's face as he held back tears, and I remember God's presence in the energy that filled my body.

Our moment was interrupted by a knock on the door. "It's time to go!" Margot called from the other side.

Standing in the hallway, I could hear my cousin singing "The Prayer." I couldn't believe it was finally happening. My dad and I stood at the top of the aisle and looked out to the crowd. We took a long pause to look at each other and soak in the moment before walking down the aisle.

It was the first time I was seeing the ceremony space, and it was better than anything I could have imagined. There wasn't a cloud in the sky, the weather was Seventy-five degrees, and our guests were exquisitely dressed. My designs had come to life, but it felt like a dream. Peter and I shared our vows, and the reverend announced us husband and wife!

© Willett Photo

Wedding Ceremony Advice

- **Retreat to a private space before the ceremony to relax.** I highly encourage you only bring your maid or matron of honor and whoever is walking you down the aisle. You want to have that special moment with that person, in my case, my father. Spending that time with him before the ceremony was so extraordinary. Your maid or matron of honor will be invaluable if you need to use the bathroom in your wedding gown.

- **Wait at the top of the aisle.** My matron of honor, Kristen, shared this gem with me. She told my dad and me to wait at the top of the aisle for a long pause and then look at each other before walking down the aisle. It was incredible to take a moment to appreciate all of the faces staring at us.

- **Personalize the ceremony.** Peter and I took the time to write our own vows. If you don't want to do that, at least select your own readings. I chose one reading from Genesis and one nonreligious reading from *The Art of Marriage*. My cousin even sang in Italian to honor our family heritage.

- **If you are willing, abstain from alcohol before the ceremony.** I wanted Peter and myself to be sober when we exchanged our vows. I wanted us to proclaim our commitment free of any mind-altering substance. We wanted to have the same experience at the ceremony and remember it for what it truly was.

For more photos, go to
www.thecovidbridebysara.com/post/ceremony

THE RECEPTION

Two weeks before the wedding, I met with each vendor to confirm their job and solidify the timeline. With the change of venue, many vendors forgot to update the delivery. A list of over thirty vendors made it vital to confirm specific arrival times to reserve the hotel's loading dock.

In addition to nailing down the vendor timeline, I met with The Southern Party Band to discuss the emcee script for the evening. I wanted to meet with Billy, the band leader, to practice the pronunciation for introductions, when to announce the traditional events, and confirm that he could play the first dance music files I sent to him.

As we were concluding our meeting, Billy brought up the stage, "I see that you have a sixteen- by twenty-four-foot stage planned for us. In our rider, we request a stage that is twenty-eight feet wide and twenty feet deep."

"Yes, I don't think there is space in the ballroom for a larger stage," I cautioned. "I will check with Pierre, the event coordinator, and get back to you."

"We are holding to our stage requirements with COVID," Billy explained. "I need to provide a safe environment for my band members so they can stand at least six feet apart."

I was worried the band would quit if I couldn't meet their COVID requirements. He'd had the ballroom floor plan for months, and this was the **first** time he'd expressed this concern. I couldn't quite buy into the idea that a slightly larger stage would provide a safer environment when his band would be performing in a room with over two hundred and fifty guests. I jumped through hoops to fulfill every other specific request the band asked for, between a private dressing room, hot vegan meals, and a case of Fiji water.

Right away, I called Pierre to ask if expanding the stage was possible. In a French accent, Pierre uttered, "There is no way to have a stage that large in the ballroom. I can't block the service entrances."

"Can you please let me know if there are any options?" I begged him.

Pierre did his best and emailed me an updated floor plan. It looked crazy; the stage overpowered the ballroom. The new stage pushed the dance floor back several feet, forcing the head table against the back wall.

Reviewing the plans, I called Pierre. "I think a bigger stage ruins the entire flow of the room. What do we do? I want the band to have enough space to perform!"

Pierre warned me, "Sara, the band will ask for the world. It's not a concert; it's a wedding. They may want a bigger stage, but this event is not about them. Let's keep our original plans."

I agreed with Pierre. At the end of the day, my vendors needed to develop creative solutions on their own. I had done everything in my power to make our wedding possible, and it was their turn to step up to the plate.

One week before the wedding, I thought I had finalized the interior designs of the ballroom until Margot texted me.

Margot: *I think an all-white dance floor will look better than the black and white. What do you think?*

Sara: *I think you're right. Is it too late?*

Margot: *No, I was able to find one.*

Sara: *OK, let's switch it. But only if we can add a monogram to the center!*

I had been ignoring my gut feeling about the black-and-white dance floor, and this was a sign from God. The dance floor company emailed me a quote with a twelve-by-twelve-foot gold monogram, but something felt off. Our dance floor was only twenty-by-twenty square feet, meaning the monogram would take up forty percent of the dance floor. I sent a request for a ten-by-ten-foot monogram and was able to cut the price by hundreds of dollars.

Ironically, on my wedding day, I didn't care about **any** of the details I had carefully pulled together over the past many months. Peter and I had a fairytale ceremony, and nothing could ruin our night.

Well past 6:00 p.m., neither Peter nor I had yet had a sip of alcohol, as we were holding off until after we performed our first dance. I went through the trouble of finding a new gown I could dance in after paying for twenty-five private dance lessons, and we weren't going to waste the time and effort. Our choreography had complicated footwork and ended with a lift. The last thing I wanted was to botch the dance by indulging in a cocktail on an empty, nervous stomach.

Once our ceremony ended, Peter and I posed for family photos and left the cocktail hour to change outfits. While Margot was escorting us to the bridal suite, she stopped outside the ballroom to show it off before it was overcome with guests. "Are you ready to see your ballroom?" Margot beamed, throwing open the doors.

I couldn't believe my eyes. The ballroom looked nothing like I remembered. It was elegant, refined, and exactly what I dreamed it could be...without knowing how it would turn out in reality. Peter and I no longer felt as if we were standing in an ordinary ballroom in Georgia. Instead, we felt transported back to our trip to Paris.

The first thing that caught my eye was the opulent ivory drapery hanging from the ceiling and behind the stage. The lighting was soft and balanced between the floor lights, candlelit tables, and glimmering chandeliers. There was harmony yet interest between the variety of linen textures and floral arrangements. The balance between high centerpieces and low and lush arrangements made for a lavish effect. Our white dance floor had our gold monogram in the center, generating the sophisticated look I had hoped for. Our four-tier cake dripped with peonies and roses between each layer.

My favorite part of the ballroom was our head table. It was picturesque with a spectacular flower garland draping across the twenty-two-person table. The backdrop was the green ivy boxwood wall framed with ethereal roses, and the center held the neon Trelenberg sign.

Last, I admired the place settings. I'd rented gold-rimmed everything: chargers, wine glasses, champagne glasses, water glasses, and flatware. Our circular menu fit seamlessly in the center of the charger. At each place setting, there was a box of gold matches embossed with *the perfect match*. Each detail was complementary, and the ballroom was flawless. Peter and I wandered around, holding hands in utter amazement.

"It's six thirty." Margot snapped us out of our daydream. "It's time to change!"

We headed upstairs to the bridal suite, and my emotions shifted from elated to anxious. I couldn't understand why I felt worried about performing my dances with Peter and my dad. I used to perform songs, dances, monologues, and presentations all the time, but since COVID, I hadn't been in the spotlight, and I felt off my game.

I changed into my nude character shoes and flowy tulle gown. Peter traded his white tux dinner jacket for a black one with a shawl collar. Before we knew it, we were standing in line behind our bridal party to be introduced to the ballroom. I can still feel the butterflies in my stomach, and my heart skipped a beat when I heard, "For the first time, I present to you, Mr. and Mrs. Peter Trelenberg!" Our guests rose to their feet and cheered us on. Just like we practiced, Peter and I locked eyes and stayed in character while he escorted me to the center of the dance floor.

Every eye was on us. The music started, and so did we. Our first few steps were stiff, so through my smile, I whispered, "Peter, you have to dance, just like we practiced." After that, we loosened up.

I was never able to rehearse the dance in my gown, so I had no idea how it was going to move. The first quick spin, I grabbed the top of my head to make sure my headband was still intact. I felt my dress rise on the second set of three quick spins, and I grabbed it to make sure my thighs weren't showing. I realized how hesitant that made me look, and thought, *whatever happens, happens, even if I have a Janet Jackson Superbowl moment.* Other than my two slight adjustments, we nailed the dance. The crowd went wild, and my bridesmaids threw their bouquets onto the dancefloor.

Peter and his mother shared their dance while his mother cried.

Finally, my dad and I performed our dance to "Vienna" by Billy Joel. Usually, my dad dances a little faster than the beat, but on the night of the wedding, he had rhythm and confidence. As much as I enjoyed performing for our guests, I was relieved for that part to be over.

The rest of the night unfolded like a movie. My dad gave a speech that brought the entire room, including our new family members, to tears. Following the speech, my godfather Sal blessed the food in Italian. After that, people hit the dance floor while dinner was being served. Even with the limited stage space, the band was able to put on an encore-worthy performance. People never dance before dinner at weddings, but the band brought people to their feet. After a year of lockdowns and isolation, people were pumped to celebrate the first wedding and ready to party!

Toward the end of dinner, my maid and matron of honor gave the most flattering speeches. I couldn't have hired professional actresses to share such kind and heartfelt words, even though they were a little lengthy. Peter's brother nailed the best man speech with the appropriate amount of humor and just enough sentiment. We danced the rest of the night away, and Peter and I did our best to stick together instead of trying to entertain everyone else.

Our band interrupted the dancing only for a moment to cut the cake, toss the bouquet and garter, and call my family to the floor to dance the Tarantella, an Italian tradition. Our guests danced up a sweat, and I had blisters on the backs of my heels to prove it. I should have ditched my shoes like the rest of the women, but I was too in love with my sparkly Jimmy Choo heels to take them off. They were far easier on my feet than the other twelve contenders I tried on in the shopping process.

At the end of the night, we had our dramatic send-off with thousands of rose petals, cold sparklers, and an old-fashioned Rolls-Royce. In our eyes, our wedding was epic. Even our wedding night was magical (if you know what I mean). Dad, if you're reading this, forget I said that.

© *Willett Photo*

Reception Ceremony Advice

- **Don't be scared to incorporate speeches.** The weddings I've been to lately have omitted the speeches and treated the evening like a big party. It's not just any party, it's a wedding, and I want to hear from the important people in the couple's lives!

- **Communicate with the wedding party about the head table.** Our head table could only seat twenty-two guests, which was not our entire bridal party. Instead of trying to fit just bridesmaids and groomsmen, we let our bridal party sit with their dates. Our head table had five of my bridesmaids plus their dates and five groomsmen plus their dates. My bridesmaids preferred to sit with their dates instead of dateless at our head table, especially since they were with me all day. Talk to your wedding party to decide what's a good fit for your head table.

- **Stick together!** Make a pact with your **new** spouse that you won't separate from them during the reception. Peter and I tried to be glued at the hip, and we still got pulled in different directions. If you don't actively try to stick together, you won't see your groom (or bride) at all. You want to remember your wedding with your spouse, not just the wedding itself.

- **Include as many traditions as you want!** You don't have to skip the bouquet and garter toss just because it's not cool anymore. Peter and I love traditions, so we opted to do them all. In addition to the standard American wedding traditions, I incorporated Italian wedding traditions, too. Look at your family history and find the culturally significant traditions that work for you.

For more photos, go to
www.thecovidbridebysara.com/post/reception

© *Willett Photo*

THE THINGS THAT WENT WRONG

My wedding was a dream. I was on cloud nine. You hear brides say things like, "It was the happiest day of my life," and "I felt like a princess." All that cheesy crap is true! **May 8, 2021, was the best day of my life.**

Sunday morning after the wedding, I woke up bright-eyed and bushy-tailed, ready for the family brunches, despite the fact I slept a total of seven hours over the past two nights. I was running on adrenaline and couldn't get over how the weekend unfolded like a fairy tale.

Monday morning hit like a ton of bricks, but I stuck to my schedule and hand-addressed over one hundred and fifty thank-you notes and stuck them in the mail while Peter was at work. On Tuesday, Peter and I got married in the Catholic church, and by Wednesday, I had returned rentals, cleaned up the decorations, unpacked wedding gifts, and stored items in my parents' basement until we figured out what to do with our new kitchen gadgets and home décor.

By the end of the week, my mother and wedding planner let the cat out of the bag. **Not everything went according to plan** on the big day. Fortunately, I had a wedding planner who did her best not to shed light on any mishaps during the event. I knew there were a few hiccups during the wedding, but all the good elements masked the problems.

It's a delusion to believe that your big day will somehow be free of imperfections. Engaged women can't help but attend a wedding and take note of experiences that were negative or inconvenient and say, "That won't happen at **our wedding.**" I hate to break it to ya, but you can't outsmart mishaps, even with wedding planning. You can only try to not make the same mistakes as brides before you.

Inevitably, something will go wrong, whether that be rain on your wedding day, an underestimation of how much cake you ordered, or an embarrassing family member. This is not me telling you to dial down your pre-wedding groundwork; you have to be okay with letting go on your wedding day. It's too late to fix, alter, rearrange, or confront anyone. It's out of your control.

MISHAP #1—WELCOME GIFTS MIA

The NOVA Hotel forgot to distribute most of the seventy-five welcome gifts to our guests as they checked in. You are well aware of the blood, sweat, and tears that went into preparing and transporting those gifts, and more than half of our guests didn't receive one.

The hotel agreed to distribute them, and I confirmed multiple times with the events coordinator at the hotel just to make sure. Margot delivered the gifts to the front desk at eight on Friday morning, well before the first arrivals. The check-in desk stashed the gifts behind the counter, but there was another wedding at the hotel that weekend, overwhelming and confusing the staff on who to give a gift bag to. On Sunday afternoon, my dad retrieved the bags that never got to our guests. It looks like we'll be eating Sour Patch Kids and Voodoo Chips for months to follow.

Ask the hotel block coordinator to give you a list of guests and their room numbers and have a friend or family member deliver any welcome gifts yourself if you are concerned about the hotel's capability to complete this task for you.

MISHAP #2—THE REHEARSAL THAT BLEW

We held our ceremony rehearsal on the fifth-floor terrace at The Brantley Hotel on Friday afternoon. The way the rooftop is oriented created a wind tunnel exactly where the ceremony would take place. The wind whipping through the terrace was so strong that three of my bridesmaids had Marilyn Monroe moments, unexpectedly flashing the groomsmen.

We could barely hear the reverend talk over the wind, and my bridesmaids couldn't focus on anything other than pinning down their cocktail dresses. It was distressing and annoying to stand outside while the wind whistled, and I was afraid it was going to be as strong the next evening for the wedding.

Fortunately, the wind died down, and the ceremony was calm and quiet.

MISHAP #3—CELL PHONE VIDEOS ARE NOT ENOUGH

During the rehearsal dinner at Occe, our friends and family members gave speeches that were priceless and vastly different from the ones given at the reception. However, we didn't have a videographer to capture them. The day before the wedding, my videographer reached out to ensure we didn't need coverage on Friday. I denied his services because I didn't want to overstep the Trelenbergs' event. My mom took videos on her outdated cell, but it's almost impossible to hear the speeches over raucous laughter. If you expect speeches, make sure you have a plan to capture them!

MISHAP #4—WEDDING GUEST DROPOUTS

The day of the wedding was a little more drama-ridden. Early Saturday morning, my dad, Peter, and I received messages from guests who backed out at the last minute. It was too late to take away a table setting, and it was far too late to get any money back per person. We paid for ten guests who didn't attend.

It's not about the money. We were in constant communication with our guests at every checkpoint with changes. We were transparent about the situation and encouraged our guests to decide based on their comfort level with attending an event during COVID. We were blindsided by those who backed out last minute, and the no-shows hurt our feelings.

Life will get in the way sometimes, keeping those you love from attending your wedding. It's just good manners to be respectful of when and how you tell someone you can't make it to their wedding—the morning of the wedding is **not** the best time. Weddings are one of those pivotal moments that create a lifelong bond with someone. The older you get, the less time you have to see your friends, so a wedding is one of those events that show how you want to be a part of the other person's life.

Don't check your phone the day of the wedding to avoid any sort of disappointment or drama that could occur.

MISHAP #5—LOOKING FOR THE FIRST LOOK

Peter's and my parents missed our first look in the park. I rented a Mercedes Sprinter Van to take them to and from photos, just so they could witness our first look from afar. When I arrived at the park, I scanned the parking lot for the van, but it was nowhere to be found.

I supposed our parents were running late for personal reasons, and I didn't want to bother them in case shit was hitting the fan. I knew they wouldn't want to miss the first look, so something had to be seriously wrong. After my mom's fall, while dressing earlier that morning, I feared she was in the hospital.

Our parents arrived thirty minutes late, just as Peter and I were finishing our portraits. My mom told me that they couldn't find the driver, and the only reason they got to the park was by asking different limos in the hotel's valet line if they were waiting for the La Chapelle party.

I'm not sure where the transportation company missed the detailed schedule. As with every other vendor, I did my part in providing a document with the pick-up time, pick-up location, drop-off location, contact information, and other pertinent details. Some things are out of your control.

MISHAP #6—SITTING, WAITING, SWEATING

The ceremony that felt so blissful from my perspective had lots of glitches. Guests began to arrive at the terrace at 4:30 p.m. when the sun was relentlessly beaming overhead. It warmed up to seventy-five degrees, and it was hot in the direct sunlight, especially for men dressed in black tuxes. By the end of the ceremony, the sun set behind a tall skyscraper, and it was pleasant.

We have no influence over the weather, but keep it in mind as you plan your ceremony. I've attended outdoor weddings in the winter where I froze my butt off! Being too cold is just as bad as being too hot.

MISHAP #7—THE MISSING MATRIARCH

My mom was the only one who didn't get the message to wait in the ballroom with the bridal party until the ceremony. She claimed no one told her where to go, so she took a seat at the ceremony and lined up for it as it was starting.

By the ceremony, my mom had started to feel sore from her fall, so she didn't notice the bridal party being directed to the ballroom.

Make sure **everyone** walking down the aisle knows where to go beforehand. This includes parents, grandparents, and the bridal party.

MISHAP #8—NO USHER, BIG PROBLEM

Much worse than the heat, a handful of guests had to stand during the forty-five-minute ceremony. I made a note for groomsmen to escort guests and seat them as they arrived, but I never actually assigned specific groomsmen to do this.

I even had a note in my wedding planning binder for ushers to seat people without leaving empty chairs between guests because we rented **just** enough chairs for everyone. Without ushers, random seats were left open, forcing guests who arrived later to stand.

I hated that this could have been prevented, but I wasn't thinking about this the weekend of the wedding. Choose ushers who are not in the wedding party because the wedding party is too busy with other tasks.

MISHAP #9—WHAT DID SHE SAY?

During the ceremony, my cousin Jess gave the first reading from Genesis. As someone who hates public speaking, she did amazing, even with the distraction of Peter's fifteen-month-old niece discovering her voice in the front row.

When it was Peter's sister's turn to share her reading, she stepped on the stage and began reading before adjusting the microphone stand, which was fit for my much shorter cousin. Peter's sister had to hang over the microphone, and people in the back couldn't hear my favorite excerpt from *The Art of Marriage*.

We didn't get to rehearse with microphones because our ceremony space wasn't set up until the day of the wedding. If you are getting married outside with the same downfalls, or if you must rehearse somewhere other than the wedding venue, pack a microphone stand to practice with. If you are getting married in a church, they will already have microphones rigged up and ready to go for the rehearsal.

MISHAP #10—ABSENT ARRANGEMENTS

In addition to my bridal bouquet not being the correct arrangement, the groomsmen were missing two boutonnieres, and the grandmothers were never given their corsages. My dad and Peter's dad gave their boutonnieres to the two unadorned groomsmen.

MISHAP #11—THIS IS WHY WE DON'T SEND CHRISTMAS CARDS

After the ceremony, my family attempted to get an extended family photo. We can **never** get a group photo because someone is always missing. Even if we're all present, I can't guarantee we can take a decent one.

It took my family **fifteen** minutes to line up for the photo and another five minutes for all of us to shut up and smile. People kept yelling, "Jimmy, Jimmy!" trying to find a cousin of mine who went to the bathroom right when it was time for our group shot.

When it was the Trelenbergs' turn to get a family photo, they all lined up quickly and quietly and got their photo done in five minutes. Peter had just as many family members there as I did! My family has always been dysfunctional. Case in point.

If your family is harder to wrangle for group photos, let your photographer know so they can direct.

MISHAP #12—YOU'LL HAVE THE WHAT?

I should have known that something was up when I kept asking my friends to grab me The Rosie from the bar, and they looked at me like I was **nuts**. Each time, my friends would bring me a different pink cocktail, and each one tasted worse than the last.

I spent an hour with a mixologist to concoct a signature cocktail that would taste as pretty as it looked. It was made with gin (the Trelenbergs' booze of choice), rose petals, cranberries, tonic, and fresh lime. Cotton Lilies designed a signature cocktail sign with a watercolor portrait of Rosie, our Cavalier King Charles Spaniel.

In addition to the signature cocktail sign, I designed a bar menu to display our beer, wine, and liquor options. In total, I designed and paid for four signature cocktail signs, four bars signs, and eight gold frames to display them in. Not a single sign made it to the venue. Cotton Lilies forgot to check the boxes passed off to my wedding planner to take to the venue. Those were the only two boxes I did not pack myself.

Our guests had no clue we had a signature cocktail, and no one had any idea what options were available at the bar. I took time deciding on the bar menu, and I could have opted for bottom-shelf selections because no one knew what was available to order anyway.

MISHAP #13—MUSICAL CHAIRS

Whoever was in charge of placing the table number signs did not refer to the floor plan. For instance, table one on the floor plan had a sign for table five. The escort cards ensured the right people were sitting together, just not at the right place in the ballroom.

My mom, Vivienne, and I had frittered away hours creating an impeccable mix and flow of tables and guests—all ruined by a careless mistake. Family members who were supposed to be close to the dance floor ended up in the back of the ballroom and couldn't see our first dance without standing.

MISHAP #14—UP IN FLAMES

There are always one or two crazy family members at every wedding. Mine happened to be my brother Rob. When my dad was giving his speech, I couldn't focus because my brother was walking on his hands and knees, recording my dad with his iPhone. I had to stop myself from watching Rob and focus on my dad.

God must have been watching over me because Rob backed into a massive stage light. It wobbled back and forth but didn't fall over on the table or the guests standing behind it. Shortly after I watched Rob **almost** kill innocent guests with a heavy spotlight, he came to the head table to congratulate Peter and me.

Rob was drunk and talking dynamically with his hands. He accidentally knocked over a tall cylinder candle votive without noticing. I caught the hot glass in midair, moments before it would have set the flower garland up in flames.

© Willett Photo

MISHAP #15—MISSED PHOTO OPS

I rented a photo booth so guests could take home a printed photo from the evening. The photobooth was outside the ballroom for spatial reasons, and the majority of our guests didn't know we had it. I wish I had put it next to the guestbook table instead!

I also stationed a seating vignette on a small patio outside the ballroom. Only the smokers got to enjoy this French-looking seating area with pillows that matched our table linens. Peter and I didn't even get to see it! Take extra time to design the layout of your event to make sure the meaningful details are not missed.

MISHAP #16—PARTY FOUL, I MEAN FAVOR

At the end of the night, Margot stationed one hundred and fifty party favors by the door. Guests took one for themselves instead of one per couple, quickly diminishing the stash. I won't call out names, but some guests took multiple bottles. I'm glad some of our guests got to enjoy our party favors.

If you are giving away mini bottles of booze, have one per person and arrange careful distribution!

MISHAP #17—FIRE AWAY

Peter was most disappointed with the grand finale send-off at the end of the night. The flower petal exit was great, but there were no flames when Peter and I walked toward our Rolls-Royce! The cold sparklers didn't ignite until we drove away.

I don't blame anyone for this because I know how confusing they are to operate. On the Thursday before the wedding, GA

Special FX dropped off the machines and gave Margot and me a quick tutorial. You have to charge them, insert powder, use a time card, and a few other steps I don't remember. The company advised practicing before the wedding, but we ran out of time.

MISHAP #18—LET THEM EAT CAKE

Peter and I never got the top of our cake to freeze and eat a year later. When I asked the venue if they saved the top layer of our cake, they never got back to us with a response. We loved the wedding cake we chose—pink champagne with a light vanilla buttercream. We had three cake tastings before landing on this combination.

We were told many times that the cake doesn't taste good a year later, but that's not the point. We would have eaten it that week. No one says it's bad luck to eat the top of your cake before your first-year anniversary! If you know us, we would never turn down an occasion to eat cake.

THE END

With international destinations severely limited, I rebooked our two-week honeymoon to Hawaii a month before the wedding.

With the exception of taking COVID tests and having the resort largely to ourselves, our honeymoon felt relatively normal. We stayed in Oahu the first week. We took a helicopter tour, hiked Diamondhead, visited Pearl Harbor, explored the North Shore, went to a luau, and tasted every Mai Tai on the island. In Maui, we snorkeled the reefs, drove the road to Hana, and relaxed at the poolside.

On the last day of our honeymoon, I woke up to a text from Delta Airlines.

DELTA: *Your flight Delta 366 is now departing at 9:53 p.m. on May 30 from OGG (Maui) to SLC (Salt Lake City). Please visit delta.com to reschedule your connecting flight.*

The departure time was three hours later than originally scheduled. There was hope; our honeymoon didn't have to come to an end just yet. Often, when a flight is rescheduled early in the day, there is a great possibility it will be canceled altogether. Our flight had a connection in Salt Lake City, with limited ability to hop on another connecting flight. Peter had never flown on a lie-flat bed before, so I'd drained my Delta SkyMiles account and splurged on two first-class seats for the honeymoon. If Delta couldn't rebook our first-class tickets, we may have to reschedule for the next morning. I mentioned the idea to Peter, but unfortunately, staying another night was not an option. We could narrowly afford our first week in Hawaii.

Peter groaned. "I need to get back to work to pay for these past two weeks of extravagant dinners and cabana rentals." He was right; we couldn't continue to live in our honeymoon fantasy. I rebooked our tickets for the last seats available on the back of the bus without reclining seats or dinner service. The downgraded seats were a symbol of the looming reality.

We spent our remaining hours on Wailea beach, enjoying every last sunburned second. At 4:00 p.m., we left with just enough time to shower, throw our wet swimsuits in our bags, and check out moments before they could apply an exorbitant late-checkout fee.

Our hotel held our suitcases while we sat at the bar, sipping our last cocktails as honeymooners. I was unbelievably sad. A heavy cloud hung over that last magical sunset. It's not that I wasn't eager to get home to the creature comforts of our apartment or cuddle up with our sweet puppy, Rosie, but I was sad this story was coming to an end.

On May thirtieth of the previous year, Peter and I had no idea what a whirlwind our engagement year would become. We didn't realize we hadn't secured the wedding venue we thought we'd booked months prior. We could not have imagined we would cancel our engagement party in August, our young venue coordinator would tragically die, or the wedding planner we loved would ghost us. We didn't know we would nearly miss the opportunity to be married in the Catholic church due to a minor misstep in the premarital counseling requirement.

Exactly one year prior, we were living with my parents with no idea where we would make our first home. Peter had no clue he would be committing to months of dance lessons, where we would get on each other's last nerve when I pushed too much in practice. We didn't know I would buy the world's most uncomfortable wedding gown and have to buy a new one to dance in mere weeks before the wedding.

On May thirtieth of 2020, we wouldn't have believed you if you told us we would have to replan our wedding ceremony in three short weeks. Our families didn't know they would have to help us individually text every guest with updates as the venues continued to evolve. Lastly, we wouldn't believe that a year later, COVID would keep us from traveling to Europe for our honeymoon.

Most importantly, I didn't know a year's worth of challenges would lead to a magical weekend. Hands down, marrying Peter was the happiest day of my existence.

The past year unraveled faster than a cheap Forever 21 tank-top in the wash; I was sad to let go of the planning, work, and anticipation required to host the wedding of our dreams and the honeymoon we deserved. Despite every obstacle we faced, I wouldn't change any of it.

As I sipped my last cocktail in Maui, I would have done anything to press pause on life. I wasn't ready to let go, and delaying our return flight felt like a solution. When Peter and I returned home, I would no longer be The COVID Bride. I would no longer be the twenty-something engaged to a handsome bachelor. We wouldn't have showers, parties, and events in our honor to look forward to. C'mon, we loved the attention. When we returned home, we would be a typical married couple. I feared my "coolness" would wash away the second I boarded the return flight to Atlanta. I felt older but not any wiser.

I knew on the other side of that gate the real world began. Our conversations would no longer entail which flower or cake flavor we preferred. Instead, they would revolve around budgeting, savings accounts, and how to stretch two hundred dollars' worth of groceries across a week of home-cooked meals. The responsibilities of building a life together wouldn't be easy, but if I learned anything from our past year of challenges, each hardship we faced would only make our story more interesting and present opportunities to fall deeper in love and faith.

Our wedding story was coming to an end, but as you're reading this, Peter and I have already embarked on an entirely new novel.

It's been an absolute pleasure sharing my story with you. To every COVID bride or future bride out there, I am not going to tell you to enjoy the journey. Instead, I am going to tell you to **feel** every emotion.

- It's okay to be disappointed if something you worked on doesn't come to fruition.

- It's okay to get sad if someone you thought was going to be there for you lets you down.

- It's okay to be anxious and not sleep a wink the night before your wedding.

Disclaimer: I am not saying it is okay to yell at your wedding planner or bitch out your bridesmaids. I am offering you the advice to feel every emotion this journey presents.

For Peter and me, I am unsure what God has in store for us, but if it is half as eventful as the past year, I'll be back with another book to share with you.

Much love,
The COVID Bride

For more photos,
go to www.thecovidbridebysara.com/post/theend

ACKNOWLEDGMENTS

First and foremost, I want to thank my grandma for telling the entire town I was writing a book back when my manuscript was nothing but notes on my phone. Undoubtedly, her support gave me the confidence to move forward.

Next, I'd like to thank my incredible husband for always supporting my crazy goals and dreams.

I'd also like to thank my parents, who have always been and will always be main characters in my life. Without them, this book would not be possible.

To my bridesmaids, thank you for your friendship over the years. I truly love every single one of you like a sister.

A huge thank you goes out to my wedding crew—Melissa, Kristen, Caroline, Daniel, Benny, Marc, and so many more. I can't thank you enough for bringing the wedding of my dreams to life.

Also, thank you to the people who prepared me for the wedding: Glenn for whipping me into shape, Katelyn for the natural spray tans, Sam for facials that made my skin glow, Desiree for keeping my hair healthy, Dr. Pare for the pre-wedding skin routine, and Jolie Nails for my flawless manicure. My beauty crew is the real unsung hero!

Shareen, thank you for the hours spent working alongside me to edit this novel. You've taught me so much about creative writing, and I hope to continue to work with you in the future. Another shout out to my wonderful friend and photographer Lane; thank you for capturing images that embodied my vision.

I'd also like to thank my entire family for their unconditional love and support. Mam, I wish you were able to be a bigger part of this story. I love you.

To the man upstairs, thanks a million for the continued blessings.

CPSIA information can be obtained
at www.ICGtesting.com
Printed in the USA
BVHW030737310122
627608BV00006B/321